THE
WRITER'S
PROCESS

Getting Your Brain in Gear

Anne H. Janzer

The Writer's Process

Getting Your Brain in Gear

Copyright © 2016 Anne H. Janzer

Cuesta Park Consulting

Mountain View, CA

PRINTED IN THE UNITED STATES OF AMERICA

ISBN-10: 0-9864062-2-8
ISBN-13: 978-0-9864062-2-5

PRAISE FOR
THE WRITER'S PROCESS

"Research-based, hands-on, step-by-step wisdom that can help you wrestle with the lizard brain. Certain to help thousands of would-be writers write."

Seth Godin

Author, *The Icarus Deception*

"Creativity isn't a mystery and neither is writing. *The Writer's Process* gives readers a clear-cut process to distill their ideas and get them down on paper more quickly...but also more powerfully."

David Burkus

Author, *The Myths of Creativity*

"If you've ever struggled with getting your ideas out of your brain and onto something others can access (and who hasn't?), Anne's book is for you."

Ann Handley

Author of the WSJ bestseller
Everybody Writes (Wiley)

"Finally someone has taken the cutting edge research in cognitive science and applied it to the craft of writing. Anne Janzer's *The Writer's Process* will give you practical advice on how to beat resistance and get your writing done."

Tim Grahl

Author of *Your First 1000 Copies*

"This is a fantastic guide for anyone who struggles to get words on paper, and that includes most of us. Writing is not a process that comes naturally to everyone so if you want to make it easier, you need this book. Highly recommended!"

Stephanie Chandler

Author of *The Nonfiction Book Marketing Plan*
Founder, Nonfiction Authors Association

"If I had Anne Janzer's *The Writer's Process* 40 books ago, I'd probably have written 80 books by now. There are a lot of good books about writing out there, but this is the first to realistically offer assistance based on writing in partnership with your brain, not in opposition to it."

Roger C. Parker

NY Times-recommended design author,
Top-performing blogger, *Content Marketing Institute*

Contents

Introduction

The Search for a Better Process

Tolstoy opens *Anna Karenina* with this premise: Happy families are all alike; every unhappy family is unhappy in its own way.

When it comes to writers and their methods, the reverse is generally the case. Happy writers develop their own unique ways of working; unhappy ones face similar problems.

Writing is intensely personal. Productive writers develop strategies that suit their individual personalities and environments.

When things go well, the words seem to pour from us, and we access thoughts and phrases from the mysterious depths of our minds. Our methods for reaching this state vary; some people prefer scrawling on paper in a crowded café, others type on a computer keyboard in total isolation, disconnected from the Internet. Beyond the act of getting the words down on paper, we apply different strategies for exploring and researching, revising, and publishing.

Sometimes the work is slow and laborious. We struggle to find the right opening sentence, or beat our heads against the wall to jar loose unwilling words. Partway through a long endeavor, we question our ability to complete it. Or we end up spending hours on social media, neglecting the work that is so fulfilling for our spirits or essential to our incomes.

I blame it all on our brains.

All writing originates from the same basic tool: the human brain. Although this magnificent and convoluted organ is capable of nearly infinite varieties of thought and expression, we all share certain responses and behaviors. The mental processes that make writing fun and rewarding can sabotage us if we don't know how to manage them.

For centuries, people have searched for ways to access inspiration and streamline content creation. Whether praying to the muses or shutting themselves into dark rooms, authors use trial and error to find the methods that work for them.

What if we could apply cognitive science principles to determine our own perfect methods for creativity and productivity?

Behavioral Writing Sciences

In 2002, a psychologist won a Nobel Prize for Economic Sciences. As a pioneer of the field of Behavioral Economics, Daniel Kahneman explores the nonrational, human variable within economic equations.

Behavioral Economics is a mash-up of psychology, neuroscience, and economics that examines how people make decisions in the real world rather than an idealized marketplace populated by completely rational humans. (Finally, someone has made the study of economics interesting!) It explains why people make poor financial choices, and offers the hope that by understanding decision-making biases we might lead happier, more successful lives.

Can we do something similar for the practice of writing?

The expanding field of cognitive science sheds more light on the mysteries of human behavior with each passing month and year:

- Behavioral economists explore our irrational decisions in common situations.
- Neuroscientists examine the areas of the brain involved in various types of focus and attention.
- Psychologists study the effects of self-control and mindsets on our success in life.

What can cognitive science reveal about mental states during the phases of the writing process? Would a better understanding of the brain's activities help writers find their own ideal processes and avoid common obstacles?

I propose a new field of academic study: behavioral writing sciences.

OK, that's probably not going to happen anytime soon. Until it does, we can combine the teachings of science with the lessons of real-world experience to answer pressing questions, such as:

- Why do I sometimes become completely engrossed in the words and lose all track of time, while other times I can hardly eke out a single sentence? How can I get more of those fun and fluid episodes and fewer of the agonizing ones?

- How can I fit the contemplative act of composition into the whirl of daily life?
- Why do my best ideas come in the shower, and how can I make use of that?
- What should I do when I feel completely stuck and the deadline is almost upon me?

These questions affect every writer: the famous novelist, the entrepreneur drafting a compelling business plan, and the chemist struggling to explain her work to global business partners. The ability to express thoughts coherently and creatively through the written word is a professional asset as well as a personal attribute. It's worth cultivating.

Writing in the 21st Century

While in Boston for a marketing conference, I caught a ride to the hotel using the ride-sharing service Lyft. I mentioned to the driver that I was researching a book, which triggered a lively conversation about writing. He was an aspiring screenwriter who planned to move to Los Angeles to pursue his dream. We spoke about the craft of storytelling and the challenges of finding time to work.

That was the first of several related conversations during the conference. At a cocktail reception, a business marketer told me that she pens short stories in her evenings and on weekends. Other attendees complained of the difficulty of finding accomplished writers who understood their industries, and of creating enough content for their blogs. A respected marketing author and speaker told me that she finds the study of marketing personas compelling because she identifies as a screenwriter, and plans to pursue that craft later in life.

The world is filled with writers, and it needs still more. The best writing creates moments of communion between author and reader. A story engrosses you, or a turn of phrase resonates deeply with your own experience. In that instant, you connect with another person through words.

Modern life has not dampened the urge to express ourselves and connect with each other. Even with streaming video, Instagram, Twitter, and texting, the written word continues to connect us as people on this planet. There's still a place for nuanced thought and sentences beyond 140 characters.

The world around us interferes with the process of creating in-depth work. Open-cubicle office environments, always-on connectivity, and constant interruptions impede productivity. Even if your job has "writer" in its title or list of duties, distractions and competing demands for attention make the workplace inhospitable to creative contemplation and focused drafting. For those thrust into writing responsibilities without a strong handle on their inner processes, the situation can be unbearable.

This is both the best and worst of times for those engaged in written communications. (Sorry, Dickens.) Three trends are changing the landscape, and us along with them.

Online publishing: With the growth in digital content, everyone can now publish. Gone are the days of submitting self-addressed, stamped envelopes to magazine editors.

If you have something to say, publish your own blog. Easier still, post your thoughts on Medium, LinkedIn, Facebook, or other sites with a built-in audience. In the world of books, publishing gatekeepers are being marginalized by a rising tide of independent publishers and self-publishing.

There's a sobering downside to this state of affairs: a *content glut* affects both our business and personal lives. There's only so much time in the day to consume content. As readers, we must be more selective; as writers, we risk contributing to the noise and getting lost in its clamor.

The Internet: The Internet is a boon to writers, offering instant access to research and potential interview subjects. Yet it also serves as a nearly constant source of distraction and temptation. Jane Austen scribbled snippets of her novels on tiny slips of paper in the parlor between visitors. How would she have fared in a world of social media? One can only imagine.

The technology of writing: From pen and pencil to typewriters, word processors, tablets, and voice recognition, the technologies that transfer words from our brains to paper inevitably affect the process. Famous authors of the not-so-distant past wrote in notebooks, and cherished specific pens or pencils. Many wrote drafts longhand, then made quick revisions while typing those drafts.

While many authors still outline or draft on paper, eventually technology intervenes. We compose directly within a word processing file, which lets us restructure and rearrange as we create a first draft. A spelling and grammar checker offers instant feedback on mechanical issues. Technology may blur the boundaries between composition and revision.

Each time the world around us changes, we have to examine how it affects our inner, mental processes. Rather than railing against the open-cubicle environment or lack of time for quiet contemplation, figure out how to fit writing into your life. Put aside issues of which writing software to use or whether it's best to compose text online or with pen and paper, and examine the most powerful and important writing tool at your command—your brain.

Finding Your Own Process

Writers have always struggled with the same core issues: getting the work done (productivity) and creating something worth reading (creativity). And, unless you believe that misery is necessary for true art, aim for a third goal: making the process enjoyable, cultivating a fulfilling and happy life that includes writing.

Let's consider this our triple objective: productivity, creativity, and enjoyment. Surely that's not asking too much?

Cognitive science offers rational explanations for the practices that many successful authors employ, like writing in the early hours, on isolated islands, or in special workspaces. Without telling us exactly *what* to do, science may explain *why* these tactics work.

Science also helps us understand the problems we encounter, and where we might go astray. For example, many people struggle with procrastination, or don't identify as "writers" even though they earn their living by summoning words out of thin air. Science offers clues to the reasons for those limiting behaviors and how to bypass them.

By understanding the mental processes behind the act of writing, we can work in a way that complements the mind's patterns and preferences. We can schedule work and search out environments that suit our personal needs, whether researching, drafting, or revising. When we get to work, we can muster the type of attention and focus that the task at hand requires.

This book is not a guide to grammar, nor is it a style guide. It's not a collection of writing prompts. It's not even an inspirational book, although I hope it does inspire.

Instead, it combines the field-tested practices of successful and productive writers with insights from cognitive science, so that you might master the inner game of the craft in your own particular way. It's a practical guide to what's going on inside the writer's mind and how that affects the work.

My hope is that no matter how proficient and professional you are, you'll find insights into the way you work best, and use them to fine-tune your own processes.

I write nonfiction, so that's my baseline. People tell me that writing fiction is entirely different. Based on the diaries of famous authors, I'm not convinced. Certainly, novelists rely heavily on creativity, and may approach the first draft differently. But in the end, everyone shares similar mental tendencies and obstacles.

This book is about developing productive, enjoyable writing habits. If that sounds like a good idea, read on. No matter your genre, you'll find a great deal that applies to your craft.

The book is organized as follows.

Part One: The Inner Gears offers a quick tour of the cognitive subjects related to the craft of writing. Don't worry, you won't have to diagram and label various parts of the brain. Instead of physical structures, these chapters discuss the mental processes that are highly relevant to the act of writing, including attention, creativity, self-discipline, and flow.

Part Two: The Process, Start to Finish traces the movement of ideas from the mind to the outside world through the act of writing. This part sketches out a seven-step recipe that eerily parallels the process of baking bread. These seven steps include assembling the ingredients, shaping the content into an outline, drafting, revising, and publishing, with additional periods for rest and incubation.

Part Three: Writers in the World offers guidance for using the seven-step process in the context of daily life. We'll look at how to address common challenges such as finding time to write, overcoming writer's block, and sustaining the long effort of authoring a book.

There's no single way to write. Things work or they don't, depending on what you're doing and how your brain operates. But by the time you're done reading this book, I hope you will have found ideas you can experiment with to improve your writing life along three critical dimensions:

1. Productivity. Fit tasks to your abilities, environment, and schedules. Make progress during times you're not actively sitting at the keyboard or desk. Lose track of time while drafting. Manage multiple obligations without going crazy. Protect yourself from procrastination.

2. Creativity. Schedule incubation and invite inspiration. Learn to listen to ideas and insights happening below the level of your conscious, narrating mind.

3. Enjoyment. Create an environment that matches the work, minimizing distractions and inviting the state of flow. Approach the writing process with a growth mindset. Remain resilient in the face of setbacks and doubts.

The first step toward achieving these goals is getting a better understanding of exactly what's going on in your brain.

Part One:
The Inner Gears

Schools and universities teach the mechanics of writing: grammar, vocabulary, and the essay form. Creative writing classes teach character development and story structure. But most literature and composition courses lack instruction about the most powerful writing tool of all: the brain.

As students and working writers, we are left to figure out how to put everything together without understanding what's going on in our heads. We observe our behaviors and come up with rituals and routines, hoping for the best.

You hone the craft of writing through practice; it does not arise from understanding the mind alone. But the practice is easier and more enjoyable when you approach it in a way that complements your mind's behavior.

The chapters in this section discuss the mental activities and behaviors that are most critical to writers: attention and focus, flow, creativity, self-discipline, and mindset. Each chapter summarizes the cognitive concept and its application to writing. Most include ways that you can experiment with those concepts to get your brain in the right gear for the work at hand.

Cognitive science is a complex subject. To make sense of the various mental systems involved, I'm resorting to a little fiction. In the next chapter, you'll encounter two characters engaged in an ongoing collaboration in the writer's brain: the Scribe and the Muse.

Chapter 1

The Scribe
and the Muse

Can you become a better skier by reading a book? Unlikely as it seems, the answer is yes.

My father started teaching me to ski when I was small enough to snowplow with my skis inside his. Dad was an old-school alpine athlete who believed in long boards and sharp edges. You could spot him on the slopes by his signature carving turns. His informal lessons focused primarily on the technique of edges, weight, and stance, with a sprinkling of philosophy.

Despite this excellent instruction, I remained a middling, timid skier well into adulthood. I understood the concepts, but rarely seemed to put them together on challenging slopes.

When my children were in elementary school, Dad would visit us annually during the February "ski week" in their school system, and we'd all head off to the mountains. As this was often my only ski trip of the season, I wanted to make the most of it. One year, I read the book *Inner Skiing* by W. Timothy Gallwey and Robert Kriegel in hopes of finding clues to better performance on the slopes.

Inner Skiing describes two selves: Self 1 and Self 2. In an athletic endeavor, Self 1 is the logical, rational mind, and the part I'd been learning with. Self 2 is the *physical* intelligence that controls the body. And when you're sliding down a steep incline at high speed, the Self 2 physical intelligence takes over—in my case, experiencing hesitation and fear.

The rational Self 1 understood that, when starting down a steep bowl, the skier should lean down the hill. But when fear set in, the rational mind was overruled by the instinct to back off. And as I demonstrated repeatedly, when you lean back on a steep slope, your skis keep moving forward and you skid downhill on your backside.

The book offered ways to get these two selves working together by paying attention to and labeling how things felt in my body. It helped me understand how thoughts can interfere with physical performance. When Self 1 and Self 2 collaborated, putting the concepts into practice, I started skiing with more assurance and enjoyment.

The "inner game" series started in 1974, when Gallwey published a book titled *The Inner Game of Tennis*. This book sold more than a million copies and spawned others covering additional sports as well as music and business. Clearly, Gallwey was on to something with the idea of the two selves.

If we have multiple selves participating in sporting activities like tennis and skiing, then certainly they are present in other parts of our lives as well.

The Myth of the Rational Self

Have you ever read a novel with an unreliable narrator? You read along happily, only to discover growing numbers of inconsistencies, or worse, that the narrator committed the murder. (A few Agatha Christie readers might feel my pain here.)

We're the authors *and* narrators of our own life stories. Our thoughts provide constant commentary, claiming to own the experiences and our very identities. We may mistake our thoughts as the triggers for our actions, rather than after-the-fact rationalizations. Psychologists can prove that, like the unreliable narrator in fiction, the voices in our heads aren't telling us the whole story.

The first lesson of cognitive science is that there is more—much more—going on than appears on the surface of your thoughts.

> Your brain is like cable television, with hundreds of channels but only a few worth paying attention to.

For example, how do you make important decisions? We may imagine ourselves drawing rational conclusions based on evidence. Behavioral economist and Nobel Prize winner Daniel Kahneman argues otherwise. He suggests that often, without being aware of it, we rely on cognitive shortcuts to save ourselves the effort of analysis.

In the book *Thinking Fast and Slow*, Kahneman explains our decision-making processes using two fictional entities:

- System 1 is automatic; it relies on gut feelings, shortcuts, habits, and heuristics to make decisions, sometimes very effectively, and in other cases with suboptimal results. System 1 is terrible at assessing probability, as any statistics teacher will tell you.

- System 2 is effortful, engaged when we concentrate to compute math problems or give someone detailed driving directions. This system consumes a great deal of energy, so we avoid using it as much as possible.

Both decision-making systems are vital for our survival. The modern world presents an abundance of choices for everything from the route to take to work to the type of coffee to order. (Decaf? Macchiato? Venti or grande? Colombian or Sumatran?) We would exhaust ourselves before breakfast making rational decisions if we approached everything with our effortful, analytic System 2.

The key is understanding *when* to use each system and which decisions merit deeper analysis.

The written word is the output of the thinking mind. Productive and creative writers learn to tap into the automatic, intuitive processes as well as the intentional ones. We'll borrow from Kahneman's System 1 and 2 to create a similar two-part model of the mind.

Our Two Writing Selves

Brains are complex, interconnected networks.

You have probably heard of the left-brain, right-brain distinction. The left hemisphere of the brain lines up with our analytical and verbal skills, and the right hemisphere with creative, intuitive, and nonverbal activities.

Mapping activities to brain regions may be too simplistic for complex tasks like producing written language. According to Dr. Daniel Levitin, professor of Psychology and Behavioral Neuroscience at McGill University and author of *The Organized Mind*, "Language ability does not reside in a specific region of the brain; rather, it comprises a distributed network—like the electrical wires in your house—that draws on and engages regions throughout the brain."[1]

Knowing *where* a mental process happens doesn't tell us *how* to activate it. The brain is hidden, but we can perceive our thoughts and behaviors. Rather than focusing on exactly where things happen in the brain, let's label groups of mental processes that we can activate when needed.

On the one hand, writing requires focus and discipline. We'll refer to the mental systems behind these behaviors as the **Scribe**. In ancient times, scribes were the people who wrote things down. In societies in which few people knew how to read, the skill of writing itself was highly valued. Scribes were not always the authors of the words they recorded.

Within each of us, the Scribe summons our verbal skills to find the right words, assembles them in grammatically correct sentences, and creates sensible structures. The Scribe manages deadlines and gets the work done.

But writers also access intuition, creativity, and empathy. These processes are the domain of the **Muse**.

No matter what genre you work in, the Muse fills a critical role, finding unexplored connections and fresh ways of approaching subjects. The Muse accesses the freewheeling, associative parts of the mind to uncover impressions and infuse our words with vivid detail or inspired metaphors.

I don't mean to suggest that writers suffer from multiple personality disorder. Rather, our minds are complex assemblages of connections, glued together with dynamic shortcuts and working in ad hoc systems. By understanding the various contributors to the process, you can figure out how to deal with them. The Scribe and the Muse are shorthand labels for describing intentional and intuitive mental processes. As the chapters that follow explore topics of creativity, attention, flow, and self-discipline, we'll look at how the Scribe and Muse participate in these subjects.

Schools typically teach lessons that apply to one system at a time.

- Academic instruction favors the analytical, intentional processes. The Scribe learns the essay form, grammar, spelling, and sentence construction.
- Creative writing programs offer advice that applies to the Muse, such as using prompts to spur original thoughts.

We learn through experience how to make the two systems function well together, when to engage each, and how to keep them from interfering with each other. When the Muse and the Scribe collaborate, the work becomes fast, fluid, and fun.

Writing with Both Minds

This book could have been titled *Writing Fast and Slow* to pay homage to Daniel Kahneman's two selves. Just as we depend on the two decision-making systems to survive, our successful careers depend on balancing the Scribe and the Muse. When the two don't work together well, the writer suffers.

Consider the tortured novelist, forever toiling in obscurity on a manuscript that never finds its way into readers' hands. This writer lives almost solely in the domain of the Muse (the intuitive and impulsive), without the discipline of the Scribe.

If you are all inspiration and creativity with no discipline and focus, then your wonderful ideas never make their way from the brain to the world. And, to be completely honest, not everything the Muse comes up with is practical or worthwhile. The Scribe functions as a critical filter.

However, working as a Scribe can be very dull without input from the Muse. If you do not tap into the intuition of your inner Muse, the effort of composing may be difficult and tedious. You have to find the right words and struggle to understand the reader's perspective through sheer determination.

You can work this way, but it's not much fun.

To be a happy and productive writer, you need to switch gears between the Scribe and the Muse gracefully. But they often get in each other's way.

Have you ever found yourself staring at the blank page, focusing intently to find the perfect word or the best way to approach a certain topic? The harder you try to summon the answer through sheer willpower, the more frustrating the experience. Then you go do something else, and the right word or approach pops into your head. The effortful focus of the hardworking Scribe blocks the input of the Muse, which only gets a word in edgewise when you give up on the task.

Or, you try to work on a dull task and other, unrelated thoughts keep popping into your head. That's the bored Muse, pushing the Scribe aside.

To streamline your writing process, you need to know when and how to access each of these mental systems. That's the subject of the next chapter.

Resources

To delve into the multiple selves mentioned in this book, check out the following:

Thinking Fast and Slow, by Daniel Kahneman, is a treasure trove of insight into the multitude of mysterious ways that we make decisions.

Dan Ariely's *Predictably Irrational* debunks the myth of the rational self, while demonstrating the consistency of the automatic systems.

---

[1] Daniel Levitin, *The Organized Mind: Thinking Straight in the Age of Information Overload* (New York: Dutton, 2014), 40.

Chapter 2

Attention

Attention is the connection between our inner selves and the outer world. Focus is the act of directing our attention.

For writers, control over focus is more critical than mastery of the fine points of sentence construction or grammar. We can always find an editor to fix the grammar or word choices, but we are the sole pilots of our focus.

Why do so many authors report that they rise early to write, or stay at the task late into the night? When darkness silences the demands of the world, it is easier to focus attention on the act of writing.

The external environment cannot bear all of the blame; we are often our own worst enemies, our minds flitting to other things we'd rather be doing. With smartphones and constant connectivity, we're only one click away from friends' social media posts or the latest trending topics on Twitter.

> Attention and focus are essential skills for writers in a noise-filled world.

We cannot always control the world around us, but we can manage what's going on in our own heads. The previous chapter described the inner Muse and Scribe, two key actors within the writer's mind. We move between those systems by directing our attention.

The Science of Attention

In the book *Focus: The Hidden Driver of Excellence*, Dr. Daniel Goleman describes two primary systems regulating focus within our brains.

The top-down mind is effortful, intentional, and the seat of self-control. It exercises **focused attention**, as in "I'm going to shut out the world and work on this task for a while."

The bottom-up mind as described by Goleman is automatic, intuitive, and impulsive. Like the automatic decision-making self described by Kahneman, this system helps us navigate complex environments while preserving our energies and sanity. The bottom-up mind operates through mind-wandering, **open attention**.

Everyone understands the concept of focused attention, because we work to achieve it. Open attention happens when we daydream, or when our minds aren't focused on any particular task.

When you take a walk, go for a run, or pursue everyday activities that don't require effortful focus, your mind can enter a state of open attention. During these periods, other parts of the brain can be heard above the stream of intentional thought. Ideas often appear out of nowhere, or we suddenly remember important, unfinished tasks we had forgotten.

Society values the ability to maintain focused attention, but we rely on open attention for other critical behaviors, including:

- Noticing changes or threats in the environment
- Detecting other people's responses and body language
- Making connections between unrelated areas or ideas

You don't want to go through life without healthy doses of open attention.

Writing and Attention

The two attention systems map well to our inner writing heroes, the Scribe and the Muse.

- The Scribe deploys the top-down, effortful mind. We access the Scribe with focused attention.
- The Muse inhabits the bottom-up, intuitive mind. We connect with the Muse through open attention.

The focused attention of the Scribe gets authors out of bed in the early hours of the morning, or keeps us toiling even when we'd rather do anything other than the work in front of us. We value the ability to focus. But in our urge to get things done, we often neglect the importance of time spent doing nothing, with our minds wandering.

Open attention is how we connect with the Muse and the cognitive processes going on beneath our intentional thoughts. And our brains are filled with interesting connections. What can we offer as writers, if not our unique slant on the world? That slant includes thoughts beneath the obvious ones. Even nonfiction authors choose the right stories, metaphors, and angles, inspired by the Muse.

In his book *Focus*, Daniel Goleman makes the connection quite clearly: "Open awareness creates a mental platform for creative breakthroughs and unexpected insights."[1]

By making time for open attention, you can invite your brain to ponder and play with ideas or topics even when you're not actively drafting or making notes. This subconscious work primes the brain to contribute words fluidly and easily when the time arrives to draft.

The Muse delivers the ideas and inspiration that fuel the Scribe. Without the Muse, writing is drudgery.

Experiment with Focus

Attention is at the root of many common writing ailments. Writer's block, for example, might happen when you neglect open, mind-wandering attention and thus lose touch with the Muse. Procrastination and distraction are failures of the Scribe's focus.

By mapping attention types to phases of the writing process, you can become more productive and creative. Everyone uses different methods of balancing the Muse and the Scribe. Experiment with the following suggestions to see which work for you.

Alternate periods of focused writing with open attention. Accept that your mind *will* wander and make that part of your master plan. After working intently for a while, take a break away from the desk for a less mentally taxing activity.

Most people get more done in three one-hour blocks of work separated by breaks than in one four-hour stint.

Consider using a method like the Pomodoro Technique®, which was initially developed as a time management strategy by Francesco Cirillo. Work without stopping for 25 minutes, then take a five minute break. Use a timer to keep track of the segments. It's like interval training for focus.

Switch between the Scribe and the Muse by shifting from focused attention to open attention.

Build open attention into the schedule. If you owe someone a blog post, don't wait until the day it's due to think about it. You can probably finish it faster and with less stress if you start researching and considering the topic as early as possible. Let it sit for a day or two while you ponder your approach during periods of open attention.

I like to think of this as creative procrastination. You delay the first draft without feeling guilty, but you start thinking early, giving the brain time to work on a strategy as you do other things.

Find the right environment for focus. Some people can only concentrate in total silence. Others prefer the buzz of conversation or the hiss of espresso machines. Figure out the environment that works for you, and retreat to it when the work requires focused attention.

Be careful about what you bring with you. Even when you intend to focus, technology can sabotage your efforts. A cell phone next to you on the table can grab your attention with notifications of emails or texts. Facebook on an open browser tab can steal your focus when the Scribe is at a loss for words.

Technology is most tempting when the work is difficult. If you need to focus, put these distractions aside.

When you get stuck, take a break for the Muse. The answer to a problem often appears when you stop laboring to find it. The next time you're stuck, think explicitly about the problem you want to solve to prime your thought processes, then walk away. Find your favorite method for entering a state of open attention.

If it's late, get a good night's sleep. The brain connects and processes materials from the day during the Rapid Eye Movement (REM) phase of sleep. If you're commuting to work, turn off the radio or podcast and let your mind wander. (If you're driving, pay attention to the road, of course!) Even if an answer doesn't strike you immediately, it may arrive when you next sit down to work on the problem.

Invite the mind to wander. Inviting the Muse may be as simple as taking a walk outdoors, gardening, bathing, or exercising.

For Madeleine L'Engle, author of the beloved children's book *A Wrinkle in Time*, playing piano was the path to open attention. In an interview with famed psychologist Mihaly Csikszentmihalyi, she revealed the role of music in her personal process. "If I'm stuck in writing, if I can I sit down and play the piano. What it does is break the barrier that comes between the conscious and the subconscious mind."[2]

Navigate around the trials of daily life; let your mind wander to unresolved issues while waiting in line for coffee or sitting on an airplane. Look for opportunities to give the Scribe a break, inviting inspiration, intuition, and roaming connections. As Daniel Goleman puts it: "A mind adrift lets your creative juices flow."

Cultivate slices of solitude. The mind wanders most freely when you are not engaging actively with others, during periods of solitude.

If you live in a city, people are everywhere. But you can often find mental solitude in a crowd. Try sitting alone in a coffee shop, or walking down a city street.

Virtual companions can interrupt your solitude as well. Even when you don't see them, other people are with you, courtesy of your cell phone. Rather than being alone with our thoughts, we often reach for those tempting devices and their promise of instant companionship and inclusion. Because we are social animals, talking or texting with others absorbs our attention, and prevents the kind of mind drifting that lets the Muse work.

MIT Professor Sherry Turkle has studied the effects of our connected culture on empathy, conversation, and solitude, and summarizes her findings in the books *Alone Together* and *Reclaiming Conversation*. She claims that digital devices are eroding our tolerance for solitude. "These days, we may mistake time on the net for solitude. It isn't. In fact, solitude is challenged by our habit of turning to our screens rather than inward."[3]

For proof of this, look no further than the research study from 2014 in which study participants preferred to shock themselves rather than sitting quietly and thinking.[4] Solitude is becoming that unnatural.

Put the cell phone in a different room, turn off chiming notifications, and distance yourself from the online world when you want to experience open attention.

Resources

In *Focus: The Hidden Driver of Excellence*, Daniel Goleman has assembled a terrific breadth and depth of research on the topic of attention, and presents it all in an inspiring and accessible way.

Daniel Levitin's book *The Organized Mind* discusses the challenges of managing our attention in an information-dense world.

For insight on the impact of modern technology on solitude, and how to counteract it, read Sherry Turkle's excellent book *Reclaiming Conversation*.

---

[1] Daniel Goleman, *Focus: The Hidden Driver of Excellence* (New York: HarperCollins, 2013), 42.

[2] Mihaly Csikszentmihalyi, *Creativity: Flow and the Psychology of Discovery and Invention* (New York: HarperPerennial, 1996), 253.

[3] Sherry Turkle, *Reclaiming Conversation: The Power of Talk in a Digital Age* (New York: Penguin Press, 2015), 61.

[4] I first heard Sherry Turkle speak about this study at the B2B Marketing Forum in 2015. The research can be found in Timothy Wilson et al., "Just Think: The Challenges of the Disengaged Mind," *Science* 345, no. 6192 (2014): 75–77.

Chapter 3

Flow

On June 15, 1938, John Steinbeck made the following entry in his journal: "Not an early start today but it doesn't matter at all because the unity feeling is back. That is the fine thing. That makes it easy and fun to work."[1]

Have you ever experienced the unity feeling?

We've described the mental model of the Scribe and the Muse to label different modes of attention and work. When everything goes perfectly, the two selves work together in one fluid process that unifies the creative and productive. Ideas make their way from the brain into words.

When this happens, you become absorbed in the process, outside of time and the daily world around you.

Novelist and essayist Zadie Smith describes a state of magical thinking, during which "you sit down to write at 9 a.m., you blink, the evening news is on and four thousand words are written…"[2]

Psychologists call this state *flow*.

What Science Tells Us about Flow

Mihaly Csikszentmihalyi is the expert on flow. You could say, quite accurately, that he's written the book on the subject: *Flow: The Psychology of Optimal Experience* is the layman's entry point into his research.

Csikszentmihalyi started by studying what he calls "optimal experience" or the state in which people are most engrossed in their actions. This brought him to define the concept of flow as a state of effortless attention, "in which people are so involved in an activity that nothing else seems to matter."[3]

His research has identified nine elements that must be present for flow to occur.

1. Work that is challenging but within your abilities
2. Work with clear goals (you know what you need to do)
3. Immediate feedback through the activity itself
4. A complete focus on the action
5. A lack of distractions or mind wandering
6. Absence of fear of failure
7. Lack of self-consciousness
8. The loss of awareness of time passing
9. An overall sense of fulfillment or enjoyment

These are descriptive rules rather than step-by-step instructions. Flow may arise during any activity when these conditions are met, but you cannot force it.

Why bother seeking this special state? Because the experience itself is worthwhile. Says Csikszentmihalyi, "Every flow activity had this in common: It provided a sense of discovery, a creative feeling of transporting the person into a new reality."[4]

Flow and Writing

When working in a state of flow, you don't waste time banging your head against the keyboard, surfing the Internet, or staring blankly into space wondering about the perfect turn of phrase. If you're drafting, the words roll out smoothly. During revision, you become absorbed in the text and the process of refining it.

The state of flow connects you to the joy of writing.

Flow is the ideal state, but no one achieves it all the time. Sometimes writing is hard work—drudgery, even. You're tired or worried about other things. Perhaps you love drafting but not revising.

But when flow happens, it's worth the work. For many people, the experience itself is reason enough to write. Look for ways to structure your process to increase the opportunities for flow.

The nine elements of flow map onto to three variables within your control: the work, the environment, and your inner state.

1. The work: The first three conditions of flow relate to the task at hand; it has goals, offers feedback, and is sufficiently challenging but within your abilities.

2. The external environment: The physical workplace plays a major role in whether you can focus on the task without distractions.

3. Your inner state: The remaining factors occur within your mind: focused attention, lack of self-consciousness, absence of fear, and forgetting about time.

Writers have varying degrees of control over their work. Reporters on deadlines or college students have few options about the subjects and assignments. Assuming that you can choose projects that engross you, let's explore strategies for managing the other two variables: the external and internal settings.

Experiment with Your Writing Environment

Flow is defined in part by the sense of total absorption and focus in an activity or task. Using our two-part model, the inner Muse joins the Scribe on the task at hand rather than wandering off to other subjects.

The Muse is easily sidetracked, however, so find an environment that minimizes sources of distraction, separating you from the interruptions and temptations of daily life.

Consider some of the following strategies for getting distance from distractions.

Create separation in space. A small room with an expansive view. A "tiny house" office in the backyard. What does your idealized writing studio look like?

In reality, the space itself matters less than how you use it. Most people carve space out of their homes or offices to work, finding flow while tucked into the corner of an office or sitting in the kitchen. Some writers love retreats. Others are most productive at the community table in a local coffee house.

What matters isn't so much *where* you go as what you leave behind—the ringing of the phone, interruptions of coworkers, or a queue of unread email messages. Create distance from day-to-day distractions.

Working in a dedicated space signals to your brain that you're doing something special that requires focus. According to Daniel Levitin, "Just stepping into a different space hits the reset button on your brain and allows for more productive and creative thinking."[5]

Use dedicated writing tools. Any networked computer offers infinite distractions and temptations right at your fingertips: the arrival of an email or text message, the temptation to watch a funny video (only two minutes!), or new posts from friends on Facebook. Name your own distractions—everyone has them.

Consider creating a Spartan environment to increase opportunities for flow.

I use an old laptop when drafting and store files in the cloud so they are accessible from other computers for revision and sharing. I don't use this computer for managing social media, tracking book sales, or sending emails—only for writing. It rests on an elevated table, so I stand while writing instead of sitting at the desk. The change in posture acts as a constant physical reminder that although in the office, I am operating in a different mode.

If you use the same computer for writing as other work, consider shutting off unnecessary applications during drafting sessions. Many people use applications that black out the rest of the computer, such as WriteRoom. Some rely on Internet-blocking applications like Freedom to limit distraction during work sessions. Others disconnect altogether, turning off Wi-Fi or pulling the network cable.

Create separation in time. If you can't physically get away from the everyday environment, try setting aside specific times to write.

What would a cognitive scientist do? We have an answer, courtesy of Dan Ariely, a professor of Psychology and Behavioral Economics at Duke University. (He's also founder of The Center for Advanced Hindsight, which should win an award for the best name for a research institution.)

Ariely wrote the bestselling book *Predictably Irrational* while teaching and conducting research at MIT. Although a prolific publisher of academic research, he struggled to adopt a nonacademic tone and style distinct from his scholarly prose. Legions of readers are grateful for his struggle—we'll return to his research in the chapter on self-discipline and procrastination.

As a student of human behavior, how did Ariely find the time and space to complete his book while maintaining his academic workload?

In an interview with Roger C. Parker on the Published and Profitable blog, Ariely explained that with young children in the house, working at home was not an option. Instead, he created distinct time windows to work on the book: "In the day, I would do academic work. I would go home, have dinner, then come back to the office at 9 and work until 1 or 2 a.m. on the book. I split my life that way."

On a later book, *The Honest Truth about Dishonesty*, he split his time differently, working on the book during weekends only. In both cases, he used the same office space but shifted time. The change in time was a mental signal that he was engaged in a different type of communication.

Experiment with Flow

Psychologists have studied what happens in the brain when the subject is in a state of flow. Daniel Levitin reports: "During flow, two key regions of the brain deactivate: the portion of the prefrontal cortex responsible for self-criticism, and the amygdala, the brain's fear center."[6]

Fair enough. But how do we deactivate parts of our prefrontal cortex and amygdala? How do we draft without judgment and fear? It takes practice.

Here are a few suggestions to train your brain for the flow state.

Try freewriting. Many of us struggle to write without stopping to judge and correct. The educational system has taught us to analyze grammar; the spell-checker highlights mistakes as we make them. When we stop to try to get it right, our brains start to wander.

Freewriting is one antidote to judgment, and a great way to practice the kind of fluid connection between the mind and the hands that happens during flow. The idea behind freewriting is to get the words out as quickly as possible, without stopping to critique and revise. Here's how it works:

Open a file or a section of a notebook and give it a title like:

- Random thoughts on <subject>

- Notes to self
- Freewriting

The title matters because it communicates a commitment to yourself that the contents of this file will never be published. When you internalize this belief, you can approach the effort with less fear and self-consciousness. No one else will see these words.

Then start typing or writing about the topic, exploring what you already know and what you would *like* to know. Don't stop to censor yourself. Simply get the words out as quickly as possible, whether on a keyboard or by hand.

Demand of yourself that you continue, no matter what, for a fixed period of time or number of words. In most cases, you exhaust the easy words and obvious thoughts quickly. That's when things get interesting. To fill the void, the brain will start hunting around for other fodder. The Muse may throw in ideas or connections you had not considered. This often results in fresh avenues to explore.

If you feel truly stuck, take the part of an imaginary reader and ask questions about the topic. Visualize an ideal reader and compose a personal note about the topic. Loosen the connections in your mind and see what happens.

Most of it may be unusable. You may end up with a few phrases or sentences you can build on. Even if you discard everything, you will have explored the topic in your mind and words. Better yet, you've trained the Scribe to get the words down while balancing the contributions of the inner Muse. You're practicing a state of flow.

If you prefer a dose of adrenaline with your freewriting, try "The Most Dangerous Writing App" by a former neuroscientist named Manuel Ebert. It deletes everything you've typed if you pause for more than five seconds.

I picture Keanu Reeves in the movie *Speed*, thinking *I cannot stop typing, or all these words will die.* The pressure to keep going might work for you; experiment with it if you have trouble forcing yourself to continue without judgment.

Personally, using that application makes me focus *more* on time rather than less. It doesn't lead me to flow, but it might loosen up fluid writing.

Use freewriting in your daily practice. Many authors set a goal of a minimum number of words or pages per day. This daily milestone works well in the drafting phase of a large project. But what happens when you're between projects, or starting research on a book?

Commit to a minimum word (or time) count for freewriting during those periods. Not only does this add a flow-based practice to your daily routine, it also gives you the chance to work through problems or issues in your daily life.

You can use any software to enter and track your daily words. Fill a piece of paper or journal page if you prefer to draft by hand. I like using 750words.com, a simple cloud-based environment conducive to freewriting. The application tracks the word count and maintains a visual indicator of how many days in a row I have managed 750 words.

Silence the inner critic when drafting. Everyone has an inner editor and critic. The voice may sound polite and helpful, saying, "You'd better check on the spelling of 'principle' vs. 'principal,' as you always get that wrong." I hear my fifth-grade English teacher, Miss Machek, insisting that 10-year-olds distinguish properly between "can" and "may" in spoken language.

- Me: Can I go to the bathroom?

- Miss Machek: You *can*, but you may not.

An inner critic like that can be inhibiting. (Or is it "*may* be inhibiting"?) You need it during revision, but it puts the brakes on the drafting process by making the Muse feel unwelcome.

If you hear yourself disparaging the sentences as they appear, politely dismiss the comments. If the criticism seems valid, make a note of what you want to fix and move on. You'll have the opportunity to correct anything worth saving later.

Banish multitasking. When you imagine yourself in a state of flow, do you also see yourself checking email? Looking to see what your friends are up to on Facebook? Watching TV? Nope.

Multitasking is the enemy of flow.

You cannot become immersed in a project if you are constantly stopping to check email or fire off a text message. Most of us realize this, yet we leave the door open to easy interruptions or doing "just one thing" before returning to work.

When we do several things at once, we portion out periods of focused attention between tasks, usually in hopes of being more productive or staving off boredom. We cannot truly focus on two things at once. Instead, we alternate rapidly between them. The switching imposes a cognitive tax that adds up over time.

The brain is a resource hog, using more energy than any of our other organs. Switching between tasks burns energy that could otherwise be put to productive work.

As tempting as it seems, multitasking is *not* a path to productivity—quite the opposite.

Turn off any chiming notifications on email or social media platforms. Social media can be habit forming, and those notifications are *triggers* that prompt us back into the habit. If necessary, ban your phone from the area, and be diligent about working without interruption. Leave those other tasks for a later time. They will still be there.

Resources

The definitive source of work on flow is Mihaly Csikszentmihalyi's book *Flow: The Psychology of Optimal Experience.*

Mark Levy writes extensively about applications for the practice of freewriting in the book *Accidental Genius: Using Writing to Generate Your Best Ideas, Insight, and Content.*

---

[1] Robert DeMott, ed., *Working Days: The Journals of The Grapes of Wrath* (New York: Viking Books, 1989), 27.

[2] Zadie Smith, *Changing My Mind: Occasional Essays* (New York: Penguin Books, 2009), 104.

[3] Mihaly Csikszentmihalyi, *Flow: The Psychology of Optimal Experience* (New York: Harper Perennial, 1991), 4.

[4] Ibid., 74.

[5] Daniel Levitin, *The Organized Mind: Thinking Straight in the Age of Information Overload* (New York: Dutton, 2014), 92.

[6] Ibid., 203.

Chapter 4

Creativity

You're working on a paper or blog post and are stumped about how to approach the topic. Frustrated, you leave the office. Walking to the car, you observe the slanting rays of the sunset on the buildings around you, and suddenly a terrific opening line pops into your head. You can hardly wait to get to your desk and start exploring it.

Chances are that you have had a similar experience—if not on a walk, then while in the shower, driving home, or staring out the window of a moving train. Fresh ideas don't always arrive on cue, but often appear when you're not looking for them.

Because inspiration arrives outside of our conscious control, we tend to think of it as mysterious, granted from the heavens. The Greeks personified creative spirits in specific muses for each art form. Composing love poetry? Pray to Erato. For comedy, seek favor from Thalia, and for tragedy, Melpomene. Nine muses dispensed inspiration and support in varied arts and sciences, creating welcome order around these unseen forces.

Cognitive science suggests that those muses are embedded within layers of consciousness, enshrined within the complex networks of our brains. Intuition and nonlinear thought are inseparable parts of the human experience, through which our inner Muse operates.

In this chapter, we'll look at what cognitive science tells us about the creative process. Don't skip this section if you deal in nonfiction. All writers share an obligation to bring creativity to every piece, whether in crafting a title, identifying a unique perspective, or finding precisely the right turn of phrase.

All good writing is creative, no matter the genre.

Creativity in nonfiction may be subtler, expressed in the selection and presentation of details, so that the reader feels truly present. I read *A Woman in the Polar Night* by Christiane Ritter wrapped under quilts, so acutely did I feel the Spitsbergen cold.

Imagination may be found in the choice of metaphor. In *The Control of Nature,* John McPhee wrote of air so hot that you could lean on it.

Business writers don't get a pass on creativity, either. Michael Lewis makes tales of obscure financial instruments and corporate malfeasance entertaining and intriguing by focusing on the personalities of key players in *The Big Short* and *Liar's Poker.*

Every assignment merits creativity; your readers deserve it.

A Five-Step Process of Creativity

After studying the state of flow, Mihaly Csikszentmihalyi turned his attention to the creative process. Instead of researching in the laboratory, he interviewed famous artists, scientists, authors, and others to analyze major creative breakthroughs. He refers to their industry-shifting contributions as Creativity with a capital C.

The authors and poets interviewed included Anthony Hecht, Madeleine L'Engle, May Sarton, and Robertson Davies. No slackers in this group.

After interviewing these luminaries about their experiences, Csikszentmihalyi analyzed what they had in common and arrived at a model of the creative process in five key phases:

1. Preparation – immersing oneself in the field and its issues
2. Incubation – time in which ideas churn "below the threshold of consciousness"
3. Insight – the "aha" moment when inspiration strikes
4. Evaluation – the process of determining whether the insight is worth pursuing
5. Elaboration – working with the insight

These creative souls had spent years studying science or perfecting their art. They struggled with the nature of reality, the design of an electronic component, or the content of a poem. Their creative insights usually arrived when they were *not* actively working, giving other cognitive processes the chance to take over and make connections. Then these individuals did the work to turn inspiration into advances in science or literature. The evaluation and elaboration stages often lasted for years.

As you can see, creativity happens in five steps, not one. The idealized stroke of inspiration is one short, fleeting part of the creative process. In *The Myths of Creativity*, David Burkus defines the "Eureka Myth" as the concept that great ideas strike us like a bolt of lightning. In real life, inspiration occurs in the larger context of work and incubation.

The creative process extends well beyond the moment of inspiration.

The Incubation Effect

Everyday moments of inspiration follow a similar process, with work and incubation preceding insight. English psychologist Graham Wallas first proposed the Incubation Effect theory in the 1920s; science and practical experience alike confirm it. You cannot hope for great ideas to alight from the sky without investing time and effort.

In one study conducted by the Centre for the Mind at the University of Sydney, students were given four minutes total to come up with alternative uses for everyday objects. This task calls on a mental process called divergent thinking. (That's how a scientist says "thinking outside the box.")

One group of students worked for four minutes without a break. Researchers interrupted the other groups after two minutes and asked them to do either a similar task or a different one. Then these groups returned and completed the four minutes.

Which group came up with the most answers, demonstrating the most creativity for the situation? Hint: It was not the one that worked straight through. The group that was interrupted for a different type of task ended up with the most divergent uses. The break gave their brains a chance to incubate the initial problem while they were distracted.[1]

Sometimes interruptions can help us by dismissing the Scribe so that the Muse can take over.

Creativity and the Two Selves

How can we combine this understanding of the creative process with our two writing selves? The five-step creative process is a kind of handoff between the Scribe (with focused attention) and the Muse (with open attention).

1. Preparation – the Scribe researches and works on the subject
2. Incubation – the Muse looks at what the Scribe has done
3. Insight – the Muse chimes in with an idea
4. Evaluation – the Scribe figures out whether it's worth pursuing
5. Elaboration – the Scribe does the work to make it happen

Individual projects may cycle through these stages many times. The important lesson is this: the Scribe is critical to creativity. A good idea doesn't write itself.

The challenge is getting the two parts to collaborate and to hand off work at the right time. For that, we can take advantage of the brain's tendency to dedicate cycles to unfinished tasks: the Zeigarnick Effect.

Bluma Zeigarnick was a Lithuanian psychiatrist. She came up with the insight that bears her name in the 1920s, after witnessing a waiter who could fulfill complex orders without jotting them down. He remembered every detail about a table and its diners until the orders were filled. But moments after the table was cleared, he no longer recognized the people he had just served. His brain reserved processing for remembering the orders while he worked and released that capacity when the task was completed.

For this waiter, the Zeigarnick Effect was a job aid, no doubt resulting in bigger tips. For writers, the Zeigarnick Effect can be both friend and foe.

If you publish works in serial installments, then this effect can work in your favor. Televisions writers know that a fresh, unresolved plot twist at the end of an episode keeps viewers thinking about the series between episodes.

But unfinished problems can steal the mental energy we need to focus on work. Research conducted by Roy Baumeister and E.J. Masicampo at Florida State University confirms that unfinished tasks remain in our minds, consuming mental resources.[2]

Researchers asked students in one group to report on a recently accomplished task. Another group was asked to write about an unfinished task or goal that was due soon. Then each group was asked to read several pages of a novel.

Those students who had contemplated an unfinished goal found their minds wandering more often, and performed poorly on a subsequent comprehension test.

Part of the brain wasn't letting go of the unresolved issue, affecting the students' ability to focus.

Struggling with a problem can similarly steal focus when you write. But what if there's an upside to this? Why not take a cue from the waiter who inspired the Zeigarnick Effect and use it to work more efficiently? Prime your mind to think about open questions while you're doing other things.

Your brain is going to busy itself with worries and unresolved issues anyway—why not direct its efforts toward your writing goals?

Experiment with Creativity

Looking for ways to encourage creativity in your own process? Explore the following strategies to activate the Incubation Effect.

Embrace the "immersion" phase of creativity. Understanding the five stages of the creative process changes your approach to the early stages of work.

Struggle may be part of the process, but that doesn't mean you have to suffer while doing it. If you don't *expect* an immediate, easy answer to your problems and realize that you're setting the stage for incubation, then immersion doesn't feel painful.

Reframe struggle as the immersion stage of creativity.

When you run into problems or questions, jot them down on a list of unresolved topics. Don't know how you should open a story? Did you write yourself into a plot corner? Make a note of what you need and where you're stuck. Then think about it before you stop working, so that you can trigger the Incubation Effect and invite your Muse to pick up the thread. Start with a clear idea of the problem you're trying to solve.

Allow time for incubation. Leave space in the schedule for pondering and unstructured musing, which happens most freely in a state of open attention.

Some people insist that they only hit on good ideas under the pressure of an imminent deadline. If this is true for you, don't wait until the last moment to start *thinking*, because that shortens incubation time. If you get a terrific idea at the last minute, you may not have sufficient time to evaluate and develop it. Also, most people find it stressful to constantly labor under extreme time pressures.

Intentionally let your mind wander. What exactly were famous inventors or thinkers doing at the storied moment of inspiration?

- Sitting under an apple tree (Isaac Newton and gravity)
- Taking a bath (Archimedes and volume and the displacement of water)
- Dreaming of a spiral staircase (James Watson and the double-helix structure of DNA)

Do you see a trend? Was anyone hard at work in a laboratory or office? No. Whether or not the stories are true, they tell of people in a state of open attention or dreaming. The Scribe was taking a break.

Once you have your list of things to ponder, invite the Muse by seeking out open attention. Walk outside. Take a shower. Nap. Stare out the window. Whatever you do, get away from the desk or your place of focused work.

Get a good night's sleep. During the Rapid Eye Movement (REM) phase of sleep, the brain processes and assimilates the events and thoughts of the day.[3] It shapes connections between ideas and experiences. Many end up in dreams obliquely related to what's going on in your life.

Most of your nightly allotment of REM slumber happens at the *end* of the sleep cycle. When you cut sleep short, you cheat the brain of important processing time that feeds your creativity.

Resources

David Burkus has written a book busting common misconceptions about creativity, particularly in the organizational context: *The Myths of Creativity: The Truth About How Innovative Companies and People Generate Great Ideas.*

Mihaly Csikszentmihalyi, the evangelist of flow, outlined his five phases of creativity in the book *Creativity: Flow and the Psychology of Discovery and Invention.*

---

[1] Sophie Ellwood, Gerry Pallier, Allan Snyder, and Jason Gallate, "The Incubation Effect: Hatching a Solution?" *Creativity Research Journal* 21, no. 1 (2009), available at www.centreforthemind.com/publications/IncubationEffect.pdf.

[2] Roy F. Baumeister and John Tierney, *Willpower: Rediscovering the Greatest Human Strength* (New York: Penguin Books, 2011), 83.

[3] Daniel Levitin, *The Organized Mind: Thinking Straight in the Age of Information Overload* (New York: Dutton, 2014) 186–188.

Chapter 5

Self-Discipline and Procrastination

What's the single largest obstacle to achieving your writing goals?

Many people answer that they cannot find the time to write. But more often, the real challenge lies in making yourself work productively, rather than doing something else, when you do have a moment to write.

Procrastination and temptation are two sides of the same coin; we put off writing when other more urgent or appealing activities attract our attention. We cannot avoid certain distractions, such as jobs, families, and personal commitments. Nor would we want to. Yet, we often turn to sources of instant gratification, such as checking Facebook, chatting with friends, or watching cat videos.

Writing takes time and effort. When you are engaged on a project like a book, the payoff may lie months or even years in the future. Taking just a few hours to do something else hardly seems to matter. But many small distractions pile up into major delays.

Cognitive science comes to our rescue again.

The Science of Discipline and Self-Control

Grab one sweet right now, or wait and be rewarded with two.

That was the essential dilemma facing preschoolers at Stanford's Bing Nursery School in the 1960s. Psychologist Walter Mischel conducted the now-famous "Marshmallow Test" to identify strategies for delaying gratification. If you have ever lived with a preschooler, then you'll understand the magnitude of this challenge for young children.

The basic test setup was simple: researchers presented a child with a tray holding a bell and two marshmallows. (Some trials used other treats, but marshmallows are the most famous, so we'll stick with them here.)

After spending a few minutes establishing trust and explaining the rules, the researcher left the room for an undetermined period. A child who could wait until the researcher returned was rewarded with both marshmallows. But if the temptation grew too great, the child could ring the bell and earn a single marshmallow. Here was the choice: delay gratification for a greater reward, or settle for less instantly.

Sounds a bit like saving for retirement, doesn't it?

The children came up with all kinds of strategies to survive the wait.

- Many distracted themselves from the marshmallows by singing, looking around the room, or making up games to pass the time.
- Others focused on the results of their behavior, imagining how proud they would be if they waited.

Mischel categorized the children as either high delayers or low delayers based on their ability to wait. The ability to defer gratification calls on the brain's Executive Function capabilities—the mental processes involved in planning and scheduling, as well as controlling attention. The Executive Function develops over time, as our brains mature. Mischel's research confirmed that older children exhibited a greater capacity to delay gratification.

As Mischel's own children and their friends progressed through school, he decided to revisit the subjects and correlate their ongoing life experiences with whether or not they were high delayers or low delayers early in life. He discovered long-term implications of this simple test of self-control and delayed gratification. Children who were high delayers in early childhood tended to do better in school, careers, and personal health and welfare years later.

One more important point from Mischel's research—resisting temptation could be taught. Children coached in strategies could hold out longer. For example, researchers suggested to the children that they pretend the marshmallow was a picture by shaping a visual frame around it with their fingers. By thinking of the treat as an abstraction, children could wait longer.

There's hope for all of us.

But resisting temptation takes effort, which drains our energies for other tasks (including, sadly, writing).

Roy Baumeister, a professor of Psychology at Florida State University, has subjected people to all kinds of temptations, including making hungry students sit in front of a plate of warm chocolate chip cookies, to measure how resisting temptation drains mental energy.[1] The results are clear: we give up more easily on difficult tasks after resisting those cookies.

In the book *Willpower*, Baumeister and John Tierney sum up two key points about our mental resistance:

1. It's a finite resource that diminishes as we use it.
2. We draw on a single reservoir of willpower for all kinds of mental tasks, both important and trivial.

Scientists refer to the draining of willpower as *ego depletion*—a phrase that sounds ethereal rather than physical. Yet research has shown that the stock of willpower is directly related to available glucose in the body. The brain's mental processes run on *physical* energy; the less that's available to it, the less work it is able to do. Hence, when we're hungry, we think less clearly and are more vulnerable to temptation.

Understanding these basic facts may affect your plans. Every email that you wrestle with before starting to work drains your mental reservoir. You may need those reserves of energy when drafting or struggling with difficult parts of the work.

Self-Discipline and Writing

We don't have to speculate about the connection between procrastination and writing quality, because psychologists have researched this very subject. Instead of children and marshmallows, this experiment deals with college students and research papers.

Dan Ariely, author of *Predictably Irrational*, conducted a study that speaks directly to the challenges of procrastination and writing. With colleague Klaus Wertenbrauch, Ariely designed a semester-long experiment using as subjects students in three different classes he was then teaching at MIT. (Never trust a Psychology professor; they always experiment on you.)

Each class was assigned three term papers during the semester. Most of the course grade was based on the quality of those papers.

For his Consumer Behavior class, Ariely proposed an unusual grading strategy at the start of the semester: the students themselves would determine the due dates for each of the three papers. By the end of the first week, each student committed to meeting a personal set of deadlines. Papers turned in late would be penalized one percentage point of the grade for each day beyond the committed due date.

Students each chose their own due dates. For example, a student seeking optimal flexibility and minimal risk of late penalties might select a single due date at the end of the semester for all three papers. Interestingly, most of the students elected to space their deadlines evenly throughout the semester. Perhaps, as students in a course on behavior, they recognized their own tendencies to procrastinate.

Students in Ariely's other two classes had their paper deadlines assigned for them at the start of the term.

- In one class, the three paper due dates were distributed evenly through the semester. Students probably had no idea they were part of an experiment.

- The second class had no deadlines; students could submit the three papers at any time up to the last day before finals without penalty. They could also turn in papers earlier, with no grading benefit.

At the end of the semester, Ariely compared the scores for the three classes.

The class with traditional, well-spaced deadlines imposed by the professor had the highest scores.

The class with no deadlines before the end of term earned the lowest grades. Many students succumbed to procrastination (imagine that!) and left all three papers for the end of the term. At that point, facing competition for attention with their other classes, the students had little time or energy to put into high-quality work.

The class that determined its own paper schedules fared better than the "no deadlines" course, but worse than the class with a traditional, evenly spaced paper schedule. The students who had given themselves distributed due dates received comparable grades to the high-performing class. The deadlines forced them to structure time for research and drafting, preventing the pileup of commitments at the end of the term.

But the average grade for this class was dragged down by the small number of students who did *not* distribute due dates through the semester. According to Ariely, "Without properly spaced deadlines—deadlines that would have forced the students to start working on their papers earlier in the semester—the work was generally rushed and poorly written."[2]

This research sums up three realities of the writing life:

1. Nearly everyone procrastinates.
2. Waiting until the last moment degrades the quality of the work.
3. Deadlines are an effective defense against procrastination.

The lessons are clear. Make firm commitments to counteract the dangers of procrastination, and schedule time to produce high-quality work.

Experiment with Self-Disciplined Writing

Willpower is a fixed and finite resource, so save it for writing. To conserve mental energy, find environments that minimize distractions.

Here are a few strategies many successful authors use to reinforce self-discipline and battle procrastination.

Establish a daily writing practice. You've heard it before, but it merits repeating. Commit to a daily writing objective, whether a minimum number of words, a page count, or a certain amount of time spent in research and note-taking. This approach breaks down the work into manageable daily doses, making it easier to achieve before depleting your willpower reserves.

Remember that you exhaust willpower through the course of the day and as your physical fuel depletes. The research makes a compelling argument for writing first thing in the morning, after breakfast but ahead of potential distractions.

Work before going online. Pledge to work for an hour or meet a minimum daily objective before connecting to email and social networks each day. This suggestion comes from Deborah Underwood, the author of several enchanting children's books, including *The Quiet Book*, *Interstellar Cinderella*, and *Here Comes the Easter Cat*. She's one of the most creative people I know.

Deborah is active on Facebook and involved with several online communities of authors. She enjoys the connectivity, but finds that it can steal hours from the day and splinter her focus for creative work.

Cutting off the Internet isn't practical for authors who promote their own platforms. To reclaim energy for creativity, she committed to working for one hour each morning before going online. She shared her goals with a group of friends who made a similar pledge to do an Internet-free hour of work every day.

For Deborah, this practice ensures that she does a session of creative work each day when her mind is freshest, least distracted by the decisions and potential derailments of email and social media. Her actions prioritize the work of writing ahead of other urgent tasks, such as arranging school visits and corresponding with editors. And the practice transforms social media from a distraction into a reward and support system for delaying gratification.

Learn to love deadlines. If you have no externally imposed deadlines, make them up. Remember Dan Ariely's Consumer Behavior students who wrote better papers with a well-planned schedule. Commitments help us resist procrastination that otherwise cuts into critical phases of the process.

Some people rely on the pressure of a lurking deadline to motivate them to write. For others, an approaching due date motivates them to keep going when temptations intervene.

If you're working on a long-term project, create many interim due dates to monitor your progress and remain motivated.

It's easy to let private deadlines slide, so share them with others. Make them public. If necessary, offer to serve as "accountability buddies" for a friend or colleague in a similar situation. The thought of having to report your progress—or lack thereof—can strengthen your resolve in the presence of distractions.

Differentiate between urgent and important. What distracts you from writing? Understand the enemy so you can limit its power when you want to focus.

For many people, the Internet is a 24-hour buffet of distraction and temptation. For others, texting with family or friends eats away at time for contemplation and work. Office environments are flooded with emails that demand attention.

All of these distractions appear *urgent*, even when they're not important. Someone is waiting for you to respond, or comment, or text them. Until your deadline looms, other tasks tend to jump in front of the writing.

Knowing that you will be drawn to the urgent, find ways to isolate yourself for periods of time while you work. Silence the pressing interruptions of cell phones and email demanding immediate attention. Consider using a computer that is disconnected from the Internet.

These strategies aren't about denying yourself, but about delaying distractions until you've done the work. Transform your favorite temptations into rewards for delaying gratification; spend time on Facebook or streaming videos in the evening if you've met your writing objective.

If preschoolers can find it within themselves to resist marshmallows, so can you.

Resources

For the story of the preschoolers and delayed gratification, read Walter Mischel's *The Marshmallow Test: Mastering Self-Control.*

The story of Dan Ariely's grading experiment comes from his wonderful book *Predictably Irrational.*

In *Willpower: Rediscovering the Greatest Human Strength*, Roy Baumeister and John Tierney describe numerous studies related to willpower and self-regulation, as well as strategies for overcoming procrastination in your own life.

---

[1] Roy Baumeister and John Tierney, *Willpower: Rediscovering the Greatest Human Strength* (New York: Penguin Books, 2011), 22–23.

[2] Dan Ariely, *Predictably Irrational: The Hidden Forces That Shape Our Decisions* (New York: Harper Collins, 2008), 116.

Chapter 6

Mindsets

As a product of the human brain, writing is particularly influenced by emotions, moods, and worldviews. Previous chapters describe how to match the external environment with the demands of attention and creativity. This chapter is about creating an *internal* environment conducive to writing.

The term *mindset* refers to a set of acting assumptions and attitudes that affect behavior; more broadly, a mindset is a filter through which we view the world.

Culture, surroundings, and upbringing each influence our perspectives significantly. Yet we can alter or adjust our mindset, as a photographer changes the filter on a lens.

This chapter discusses two mental settings that are particularly relevant for writers:

- Fixed or growth mindset
- Abundance or scarcity mindset

The binary, A/B choices oversimplify reality. Mindsets are fleeting, changeable states. Neither setting is inherently right or wrong. We might approach a financial negotiation in one way and family relationships in another. Each decision could be appropriate for the context.

This chapter discusses how mindsets relate to the process of writing. You can decide whether to examine them in other areas of your life.

Fixed vs. Growth Mindset

How do you respond when asked to do a task that you haven't tried before, such as creating a full-length book or a script for a video? Would you attempt it? If the result needs major reworking, how would you feel about the effort as a whole?

Your response to challenges and setbacks depends, in part, on your sense of yourself when considering the work, and whether you inhabit a fixed or growth mindset.

Carol Dweck, a professor of psychology at Stanford University, describes these alternatives in her book *Mindset: The New Psychology of Success.* Put in basic terms, people with a fixed mindset tend to consider their talents or abilities as set, inherent parts of their beings. Those with a growth mindset believe that they can develop abilities through learning and work.

While it sounds simple, mindset can be subtler than it seems. Of course, you understand that you can learn and improve. But when faced with a challenge, you may suddenly hear the voice of the fixed mindset whispering that you are not "good at" the task and are likely to fail. Listening to this belief limits your willingness to take on challenges.

Without faith in your ability to grow, you become risk-averse. For people caught in a fixed mindset, failure damages the sense of self.

A fixed mindset is particularly dangerous when writing, as it inhibits your ability to learn from constructive feedback. You bristle at corrections or suggestions; criticism feels personal.

With a growth mindset, setbacks and criticism become learning opportunities—painful, perhaps, but necessary. You're more likely to have a healthy relationship with editors, remaining open to feedback without seeing it as a sign of weakness.

Mindset also affects creativity. The fixed mindset shuts down exploration and discovery. You won't want to start an outline until you have *all* the answers at hand; for some people, that means that the work never gets done. The risks inherent in creative leaps become too great if they endanger your sense of self.

A growth mindset leaves room for creativity. For many fiction authors, the details of a plot only develop as the story appears on paper. Stephen King describes his general approach in his excellent memoir *On Writing*: "I have never demanded of a set of characters that they do things my way. On the contrary, I want them to do things *their* way."[1] He discovers where the characters take the plot.

Authors with a growth mindset start researching and outlining without planning everything in advance. They learn as they proceed. They take risks, and are resilient when their efforts don't pan out. Nonfiction authors consider the act of writing as a path to learning, deepening their understanding of a subject rather than simply reporting what they already know.

In her essay "Why I Write," Joan Didion confesses, "I write entirely to find out what I'm thinking, what I'm looking at, what I see and what it means."[2] She clearly approaches her art with a growth mindset.

When you engage with the subject before you have all the answers, you may find unsuspected connections, uncover different facets of the topic, and even change the direction or structure of the piece. Although these diversions may consume more time, the resulting work is often better, and the process of writing more fulfilling.

A growth mindset transforms writing into a journey of discovery.

As a reader, I can often sense if an author is exploring the topic or simply reporting what they know. When I feel that the author's understanding has deepened in the course of writing, I enjoy reading even more, no matter what the subject. Traveling the path together is more interesting for everyone.

Here's the good news: while you might have a natural inclination to adopt a fixed mindset, you can change it. It isn't hardwired.

Abundance vs. Scarcity

The preschoolers in Walter Mischel's study on self-control inhabited a world of marshmallow scarcity. They could not access an unlimited number of sweets, and made decisions based on the concept that the treats were a finite and precious resource. They operated with a scarcity mindset in this situation.

As adults, we can buy as many marshmallows as we can afford, subject only to limitations of money and sugar tolerance.

Basic economic theory is built on the premise of fixed resources. Businesses compete for a limited set of customers; products vie for our money or attention.

This approach can spill over into other parts of our lives, often with problematic effects. Researchers have found that merely thinking about money changes our behavior in subtle ways, making us less likely to spend time helping others, even with simple tasks.

One study in particular hit home for me: after looking at a picture of money, research subjects tended to spend less time savoring a piece of chocolate.[3] Chocolate! This is serious, people.

Certain aspects of our lives obey the rules of a zero-sum game that can only have one winner. There are only 24 hours in a day, or eight pieces of pizza on that plate. But many things we value do *not* abide by the rules of scarcity. Love and laughter multiply when shared or given away. Ideas, likewise, tend to proliferate when exchanged.

Good ideas multiply when shared.

When we confuse products of abundance with scarce resources, everyone ends up with less. Empathy shrinks with the scarcity mindset.

Social media evangelist and author Guy Kawasaki sums up this dichotomy nicely: "There are two kinds of people: eaters and bakers. Eaters think the world is a zero-sum game: what someone else eats, they cannot eat. Bakers do not believe that the world is a zero-sum game because they can bake more and bigger pies. Everyone can eat more. People trust bakers and not eaters."[4]

Few of us are entirely one or the other; you may be a baker in one part of your life and an eater in another.

How can you recognize whether you're an eater or a baker when it comes to writing? The scarcity mindset appears in limiting beliefs about your ideas, such as:

- *All of the good concepts have already been written about.*

- *Someone might steal my ideas unless I keep them under wraps.*

- *I need to wait for the perfect time to write.*

The more you write, the more you have to write. The process of working with ideas activates the inner Muse, and triggers abundance.

Tuning Your Mindset

You can learn to adjust mindset through practice. If you find yourself experiencing limiting thoughts about your abilities (the fixed mindset) or ideas (the scarcity mindset), use the following practices to train your brain to see the world differently.

Let your actions shift your mindset. The most powerful way to counter both the scarcity and fixed mindsets is to simply write, contradicting your belief with behavior. You've heard of the "fake it till you make it" strategy? The person you need to convince is yourself.

Don't have any good ideas, or doubt your capabilities? Write anyway. Use the freewriting technique described in the chapter on flow to discover and explore the contributions of the Muse.

If you believe that you have a fixed number of good ideas and want to save the best ones for a later ideal time, ask yourself: Will this idea still have the same shimmer in the future? Will my brain be primed to work on it, and will I be as excited about it as I am now? The future is uncertain, but the present is at hand, so write.

Recognize your unique perspective. Yes, someone has probably already written about your subject. That doesn't mean that the idea is "used up" and not worth pursuing. Shakespeare repurposed all kinds of earlier works for his plays, yet the results were unique and the world is grateful for them.

There are few original ideas left in the world. In the realm of fiction, most stories can be plotted onto a finite set of standard story lines. What matters is *how* you tell the story.

In nonfiction, the way that you share ideas matters as much as the concepts themselves.

Given the enormous complexity of the human brain, the universe of potential things to write about is abundant. If you wait for a perfect and original idea, you may never discover your unique contribution.

Resolve to learn. Whenever you encounter the fixed mindset, counter it with an active determination to learn. Read widely to fuel your brain's connections.

Work with thoughtful editors and, where possible, draw broader lessons from their comments. Rather than simply fixing the issues an editor points out, look for larger trends. For example, if you repeat phrases or sentence patterns, remind yourself to look for repetition in future drafts and explore different sentence structures, finding fresh approaches to the subject.

Do something uncomfortable. Try working outside your usual areas of expertise and see how that affects your perception of yourself.

After publishing my first book on subscription marketing, I was invited to speak at events, moderate panel discussions, conduct webinars, and do podcast interviews. For someone who had spent her life ghostwriting and working as part of a larger brand voice, this shift was daunting. Yet in each of these activities, I had a blast and met wonderful people. If I had succumbed to a fixed mindset, telling myself that I wasn't a speaker, I would have missed out on those experiences. Growth comes through discomfort.

Challenge yourself to do something different. Pen a poem or craft a short story. Even if it never sees the light of day, the work stretches your abilities and defies the fixed mindset.

Share freely. When under the spell of a scarcity mindset, you may worry about people stealing your ideas. For most of us, obscurity is a larger threat than plagiarism. The best way to counteract the scarcity mindset is to witness the power of sharing and collaboration.

Ideas operate by the rules of abundance and tend to improve as you collaborate with others and broaden your perspective. Countless people have made this book better through discussions and shared insights.

As author Steven Johnson says in *Where Good Ideas Come From*, "We are often better served by connecting ideas than we are by protecting them."[5] Instead of spending mental energy guarding your thoughts, invest it in developing ideas.

If you're creating something wonderful, go ahead and tell the world. Publish blog posts and start conversations. The risks of sharing are low and the potential benefits high.

Resources

For a description of the power of the growth mindset, see *Mindset: The New Psychology of Success* by Carol Dweck.

Happy Money: The Science of Happier Spending, by Elizabeth Dunn and Michael Norton, was my source of the world-shaking study about chocolate.

For an excellent discussion of scarcity or abundance in interpersonal relationships, read Adam Grant's *Give and Take*.

---

[1] Stephen King, *On Writing: A Memoir of the Craft* (New York: Scribner, 2010) 164–165

[2] Joan Didion, *New York Times Book Review*, December 5, 1975.

[3] Jordi Quoidbach, Elizabeth Dunn, K.V. Petrides, and Moira Mikolajczak, "Money Giveth, Money Taketh Away," *Psychological Science* 21, no. 6 (2010): 759–763.

[4] Guy Kawasaki and Shawn Welch, *APE: Author, Publisher, Entrepreneur—How to Publish a Book* (Palo Alto: Nononina Press, 2012) Kindle location 3916.

[5] Steven Johnson, *Where Good Ideas Come From* (New York: Riverhead Books, 2010), 22.

Part Two:
The Process, Start to Finish

When picturing a writer at work, people often envision a solitary individual hunched over a desktop or laptop, scribbling or typing. We summon the magical moment when the words pour from the mind onto paper or its electronic equivalent.

Drafting is merely the midpoint in a longer journey, with untold hours of research and thought preceding it and uncertain hours of revision ahead.

People who imagine that they can sit down and churn out impeccable prose are usually sorely disappointed. This mistaken assumption explains why so many people freeze up when faced with a writing assignment.

Getting the words from the brain into the world engages several distinct mental systems. When you attempt to do everything at once, these systems interfere with each other. It's no fun.

The chapters in this section elaborate seven steps of the writing process, from initial research through publication, applying the cognitive science principles of Part One and the concepts of the Muse and the Scribe. These steps impose a linear structure on a circular and iterative experience.

You may deviate from these steps or propose your own method with six or nine steps. That's fine. By isolating the phases from start to finish, you can identify and control the handoffs between the key mental systems involved in writing, the Scribe and Muse.

This section offers my personal writing process as a kind of master recipe. Feel free to alter and adapt it for your own use.

Chapter 7

A Writing Recipe

Have you ever baked a loaf of bread, or witnessed a masterful baker at work? Through a rather mysterious process of beating, kneading, waiting, and baking, an unappealing, gluey mass of dough transforms into fragrant and delectable food. Freshly baked bread is one of the wonders of the civilized world.

Baking bread is eerily similar to the process of writing.

Bread making is a mystical combination of recipe and technique, mastery and luck. The result depends on factors you cannot see, such as microbial yeast organisms that coax the dough into rising and unseen protein molecules that create structure and "crumb." The temperature of the room, conditions of the oven, gluten content of the flour, and the elevation above sea level all affect the results.

Despite these uncertainties, bakers manage to replicate their successes. They follow other bakers' recipes or develop their own and master techniques for kneading, shaping, and baking the loaves they love best.

Bread recipes vary widely based on the flour used, the amount of time available, and the type of loaf you're trying to create. Most share a basic structure, which looks like this:

- Assemble the ingredients
- Activate the yeast (or feed a sourdough starter)
- Beat and knead the dough
- Let it rise in the right conditions so the yeast does its magic
- Knead it a second time and shape it into loaves
- Let it rise yet again (the final proof)
- Bake, figuring out exactly when to remove the bread from the oven

(There's another step—cooling—but who does that when there's homemade bread in the kitchen?)

The process is rather long and ambiguous. From time to time, you go about your life, letting the bread work without you. Then you come back to punch and knead it, working hard. Then walk away again. And you hope it all turns out well in the end.

Hmm. That sounds a lot like writing—at least, it resembles the method I have developed over time. Some projects merit several cycles of revision, and others require multiple periods of rest and incubation. But the essential steps of the bread recipe map onto the act of turning raw thoughts into written work.

What follows is my personal recipe. It's not the only way to tackle a project, nor is it appropriate for every occasion. But I get the best results by sticking pretty closely to the steps. It's work, but worthwhile.

Adapt and shape this procedure for your own needs. You're already doing these steps; lining them up makes it easier to systematize and schedule the work. When you understand the phase of work at hand, you can get the brain into the right gear, calling on the Muse or the Scribe or both.

The Seven-Step Writing Process

The start-to-finish writing process consists of the following steps:

1. **Research.** Gather the ingredients. For nonfiction works, you may delve deeply into external research. Fiction may require more introspection and exploration. Although the research phase often continues even as you are drafting, eventually you have enough material to move on.

2. **Let the ideas incubate.** Leave time to activate the Muse before you start drafting. Your brain is like the yeast organisms in bread dough, breathing life into the raw materials you've accumulated. Give it a chance to work.

3. **Structure the piece.** Read through your notes and assemble a rough outline or other structure for your draft.

4. **Assemble the first draft.** It's time to dig in and create the first draft. You may have an unattractive mess when you're done, but you'll be on the path to something better.

5. **Rest before revision.** Just as you would leave the bread dough alone to rise, let the first draft sit so you can get distance. "Not-writing" is an

important stage of the process. Thoughts, phrases, different perspectives, and inspiration often strike as the draft rests.

6. **Revise and proofread**. Revision is like the second kneading phase in bread making—vital to the quality of the result. You'll wrestle with the piece from different angles, shaping it into its final form. And a final proofreading is the finishing touch.

7. **Publish**. Decide when it's time to publish. Impatient as you may be for the final product, you don't want to put your work out in the world half baked.

You already know how to write, of course, and may wonder why you need instructions. Following a defined method delivers three important benefits:

1. A recipe makes it easier to manage time so you can set and meet deadlines while juggling concurrent projects.

2. You can plan and schedule opportunities for creativity.

3. By breaking the work into its component steps, you can bring the right mental system (the Scribe or the Muse) to each task.

Managing Time

I've recently discovered *The Great British Baking Show*, a reality TV program in which contestants take on demanding baking challenges, creating ambitious projects in short periods of time.

In the Technical Challenge segment, contestants have to recreate an intricate recipe using only vague instructions. Many of the challenges require that the bakers multitask, preparing fillings and glazes while ushering a yeast dough through its steps, and assembling the final creation before the clock runs out.

Without a precise recipe, contestants struggle to allocate enough time for critical phases. The most spectacular failures often result from time management problems. As the minutes wind down, the bakers rush through the rising stage or remove bread from the oven before it's entirely done. The judges make critiques like "This is a little under-proofed" or "Another five minutes in the oven and you would have had perfection." (In a British reality show, even the harshest judgments sound polite.)

In this case, reality television mirrors life. Without a complete recipe on hand, you don't know how much time to allocate each phase of the process, particularly when working to meet a deadline. You improvise, trying to get the work out into the world and hoping that it's not under-baked.

If writing is your sole occupation and you have no deadlines, you can take all the time you need. Your challenge may be deciding when to stop and publish. But if you face external or internal deadlines, working from a process helps you get everything done with adequate time.

You can juggle different projects when you understand how the Muse and Scribe work together. For example, research one project with the Scribe while another rests with the Muse. You can guess in advance which projects will require extra revision cycles. If you don't leave enough time in the schedule, you may end up publishing half-baked content.

Remember waiting until the last minute in college to write a paper? The procrastinating college student attempts to go from research to final copy in one long all-nighter, and inevitably cuts corners. The result often falls short of expectations. Your brain needs time to explore ideas and find the flaws in your work.

The writing process isn't fun when you try to do it all at once. The Muse and the Scribe get in each other's way as you struggle to find words, get stuck, or experience the dreaded writer's block.

If we're going to invest our energies in writing, we should enjoy it.

Optimizing Creativity

You know the saying that you can lead a horse to water, but cannot make him drink? Your brain is like the horse in that scenario. You cannot force insight and intuition, but you can create the conditions that make inspiration possible.

The chapter on creativity outlined five phases of the process: preparation, incubation, insight, evaluation, and elaboration. These phases line up well with the writing recipe.

1. Research is the "preparation" or immersion phase. Immerse yourself in the ideas.
2. Incubation is the process of thinking about what you have researched and coming up with your idea or angle. (Incubation returns, repeatedly, until publication.)

3. If you're lucky, you'll experience an insight, either during incubation or when you are drafting in a state of flow.

4. Evaluation is the process of working with your ideas. This maps to the outlining/structuring phase of the writing process.

5. The elaboration phase extends through drafting and revision. Much of the hard work happens here.

Matching Mental Gears to the Work

The various phases of the recipe require different mental systems.

- The Scribe provides the focused attention for research, outlining, and revision.
- The Muse brings creative, wide-ranging attention to periods of rest and incubation.
- During the drafting phase, ideally the Muse and the Scribe collaborate in a state of flow.

By identifying the stages of the project, you can create the optimal conditions for each type of work, matched to your unique preferences.

For example, imagine you're writing a chapter of a book and need to find a great metaphor to explain a complex topic. In searching for the metaphor, call on the wide-ranging attention of the Muse to find unexpected connections. You probably won't find inspiration while staring at the computer screen.

Over time, you will learn when your best ideas arrive, whether while outdoors or relaxing with a cup of coffee.

Choose your favorite path to open attention and let the issue rest before drafting.

Likewise, when you are ready to write the first draft of the entire chapter, create your unique and ideal conditions for achieving flow: uninterrupted work time, at the time of day you feel most productive and rested, in an environment that suits your focus. Grab your favorite pen or battered laptop and shut yourself away for a while.

Use the recipe to select the ideal conditions for each phase of writing.

The seven-step process is a guideline, not a prescription. You could as easily create a process with nine, 11, or 20 parts. For example, coming up with a good title can be a step unto itself. See what works for you.

Like any great chef, you'll add your own seasonings or signature ingredients, such as your favorite place to draft or strategies for revision. You may improvise entirely, or run out of time on a project and combine a bunch of work into one burst, hoping for the best.

What matters is that you understand your ideal process and follow it, when possible, to make the work easier and more enjoyable.

Chapter 8

Research

In writing as in baking, the quality of the ingredients affects the outcome. Allot enough time for research, both external and internal.

The length of the research phase depends on the project.

- For work-related articles, blog posts, or reports, you may spend time collaborating with others to gather facts and stories.
- For nonfiction or fiction books, the research phase may take months.
- When working on personal essays or blog posts, allocate time to explore your own experiences and search for connections.

Don't stop with the obvious, direct research; look for related themes or ideas that might present fruitful associations or interesting links. Gather more information than you plan to use; your discoveries may bring up important questions you'll want to address.

When researching, dig at least one layer deeper than you plan to use.

The objective of the research phase extends beyond assembling facts to spit out later. Research primes the brain to make connections that will accelerate drafting. It initiates creativity by fulfilling the preparation step of the five stages of creativity. An investment in time exploring and thinking during this first step streamlines the rest of the process.

In this phase, you will examine sources from the outside world and within yourself. External research may include reading other sources, interviewing people, observing characters on the street, exploring settings, or finding realistic details. Internal research consists of investigating your own attitudes toward a subject, imagining how others feel, and looking for connections and angles.

Step One: Research

Who's in Charge

The Scribe

What You Need

- Focused attention for reading and note-taking
- Periods of open attention to look for connections and avenues of research
- Interviews, books, online sources
- Pen/paper or word processor for freewriting
- Tools for taking notes (Evernote, etc.)

Steps

1. Gather the research or conduct interviews
2. Freewrite to explore
3. Consolidate and review your notes

ternal Research

Start the research process as early as possible, even if you don't plan to write for days or weeks. Once you start reading and observing, you'll discover sources or notice events that otherwise might have passed you by. It's the writing equivalent of the red car syndrome; when you buy a red car, suddenly you notice how many there are on the road.

Research feeds itself: once you start, you'll see your topic everywhere.

Unless you have a clear angle and thesis ready, avoid narrowing down your scope too quickly. Begin with broad reading, then gradually pick out topics to investigate in depth. If you approach this phase with a specific set of questions, you may leave interesting angles unexplored.

When working with clients or colleagues, schedule an initial meeting to gather facts, opinions, and ideas, without committing to a specific angle. Try to initiate open-ended discussions on the topic.

Assemble the facts, thoughts, and references into a research file that you can add to easily.

Ideas will hit in unexpected times and places, so be prepared. Use online note-taking tools to capture and store links or concepts for research. For a low-tech but highly effective tool, keep a small, paper notebook with you to record your thoughts.

Research Tip: If you're researching using Kindle ebooks, use the highlighting feature to mark key passages and take notes as you read. Later, open the Kindle application on your desktop or laptop and synchronize it with the book. Open the highlighted quotes. I copy and paste these excerpts into a Word file; the citation information comes along with the text.

Internal Research: Writing for Discovery

Having perused the external sources, now turn inside. Explore what you may already know or discover potential paths for research by thinking deeply about the topic.

For many people, the best way to discover a topic is to start writing—not a draft, but notes or thoughts to themselves. Learn and discover by working with the topic.

Donald Murray was a Pulitzer Prize-winning journalist, as well as an influential teacher of the craft. In his teaching, Murray emphasized the importance of writing for discovery: "The act of writing would tell me what I thought and felt. The draft would reveal what it had to say and how it should be said. Writing was not the *result* of thought and feeling, but an *act* of thought and feeling."[1]

Use the inner research phase also to get inside your ideal reader's head, establishing empathy with the audience. Put yourself in the mind of a reader to understand their perspectives and anticipate their needs. It's never too early to consider your ideal reader.

Part One of this book discussed freewriting as a method for practicing a state of flow. It also works well for conducting research into what you already know and want to find out.

Jsing the freewriting technique for inner research:

1. At least one day before you plan to start outlining and drafting, set aside 15–30 minutes to write 750–1,000 words on the topic.
2. Open a file, and give it a name like Thoughts or Notes. The name reinforces the idea that you're not composing the first draft at this point.
3. Start typing and don't stop until you're done with your time. Ask yourself questions. Think about your ideal reader and ask the questions they might have.
4. Let what you have written rest overnight.

The next day, when you sit down to research, outline, or draft, see if you have new ideas about the material. Even if you cannot use anything in the notes file, the process of working through your thoughts may have shifted your perspective.

Finding the Point of Sufficiency

You can keep researching until you feel you know *everything* about your topic. Good luck with that! Chances are, you'll never be ready to start. At some point, you have to say, "I may not be done, but I have enough to move forward."

Only you can say when you've reached that moment.

Research is like the flour in bread. Judging the right amount of flour is a matter of feel. According to my favorite bread recipe (from Garden Way Publishing), "Flours vary greatly in moisture content, therefore it is impossible to give the exact amount you will need. Your basic guideline is to add only as much flour as you need to keep the dough f being too sticky to work with."[2]

Conduct as much research as required to work with the text. As you assemble the first draft, you might dig further into sources and add more detail. If you approach the work with a growth mindset, then you accept that you will learn as you write. What you discover may lead you to further research.

Gather and Review Your Notes

Consolidate your various research notes into a few locations.

You might keep paper journals or online ones. Some people love index cards for the satisfying visual and tactical feedback of arranging and sorting them.

For short works, I keep everything in online files. For longer works like nonfiction books, I end up with a combination of paper journals containing notes on the physical books I read and online files with notes from web research or quotes copied from Kindle. It's not a perfect system, but I have only two places to look while gathering research. Eventually, I consolidate research notes, freewriting, and quotes into online project folders

A strategy for organizing notes: Add topic headings to the research file. If you use Microsoft Word® and are comfortable with styles, apply Heading 1 or 2 styles to those headings, then create a Table of Contents at the beginning of the file. This makes it easier to navigate and peruse a massive file of notes.

Resources

Mark Levy describes freewriting applications and strategies in the book *Accidental Genius.*

Donald Murray wrote about the writing process in his book *Writing to Deadline: The Journalist at Work.* Also see *The Essential Don Murray: Lessons from America's Greatest Writing Teacher,* by Don Murray; Lisa Miller, and Thomas Newkirk (editors).

---

[1] Donald Murray, *Writing to Deadline: The Journalist at Work* (Portsmouth, NH: Heinemann, 2000), 9.

[2] Ellen Foscue Johnson, "The Basic Loaf Recipe," *Garden Way Publishing's Bread Book: A Baker's Almanac* (Charlotte, VT: Garden Way Publishing, 1979), 12.

Chapter 9

Let the Ideas Incubate

One secret of productivity is learning how to use not-writing time to advance the work. Remember that incubation is a critical precursor to creative insight.

The Scribe was in charge of the research phase. Next, invite the Muse to work with the content you have collected. Activate the Muse by pondering your topics during periods of open attention.

The purpose of this initial pause is to give the research time to coalesce in your head before you start structuring the work. Just as a baker would activate the yeast in bread dough, the writer takes a break to invite the brain to ponder the fruits of the research. If all goes well, you will start the next phase with fresh insights and energy.

Let's call this time creative incubation instead of procrastination: delay the focused work so that the Muse can spend time with the ideas. Put off the drafting, not the thinking.

Incubate the research to improve the quality and efficiency of your writing.

How long does this period last? It depends entirely on the time available and the scope of the work. You may have days or weeks. On a tight deadline, maybe you can dedicate only an hour to incubation before starting. Even if you must compress this stage, try not to skip it.

One of the objectives of this book is to help you find a process that is productive as well as enjoyable. How can you get more done quickly? Writers speak of how many words they can draft in an hour, but that measure isn't really meaningful. Most people, including clients, editors, and publishers, care about the *elapsed time* for a project as measured on a calendar rather than a stopwatch. If you can write 10,000 words in a single day but only manage to do that once a month, your productivity isn't high.

Total elapsed time includes hours spent eating, exercising, bathing, sleeping. Truly productive authors use their not-writing hours to incubate ideas. Schedule, plan, and cultivate not-writing time to make your working periods more productive.

This part can be fun. Learn to work with the not-writing parts of the process, and you may be delighted with the input you receive from the Muse. You can call on this technique anytime you get stuck, but make sure to schedule it in your seven steps.

Step Two: Incubation

Who's in Charge

The Muse

What You Need

- Open attention and solitude
- A break in time and distance
- A piece of paper and pencil, or note-taking technology (in case sudden brilliance strikes)

Steps

1. Review the notes. Focus on one or two unresolved issues.
2. Step away from the work and do other things.
3. Take note of any insights that might arise.

Review the Notes

The inspiration and insights you need will appear in the automatic, intuitive parts of your mind, during open attention rather than focused effort. It's difficult to be creative when you feel pressure to produce copy.

The problem is, this part of the mind is—ooh, a video of a drunken moose!

Sorry. As I was saying, many things entertain and distract the Muse; only a few of them will advance your writing career. Before you set off to incubate ideas, orchestrate the transfer of work from the Scribe to the Muse.

Review your research, notes, and objectives. Make a note of any problems or puzzles you haven't solved. Don't obsess or make a comprehensive list, and don't make a plan. Not yet.

The chapter on creativity describes the Zeigarnick Effect—another name for our brain's tendency to set aside capacity to work on unresolved issues. To increase the chances of this working in your favor, remind yourself of open questions before you start.

Get Away From the Desk

To begin the incubation process, remove yourself from the work environment and go someplace where your mind can wander.

- Take a stroll outdoors—walk the dog if you have one.
- Go to the gym or do something physical that's not mentally demanding.

- Take a shower.

Instead of the top-down focus you use when researching, you're inviting the bottom-up attention of the Muse. Identify your favorite methods for entering open attention. I find that I can work through all kinds of issues during a session on a rowing machine. My legs wear out before my brain does.

Once you're doing that activity, remind yourself about the topic you're working on. Don't focus on it; let your mind wander, then invite your thoughts to return repeatedly to the subject.

Capture Any Insights

During the incubation process, you may discover connections that you want to pursue or ideas to explore in writing. You may hit on a better way to structure part of the piece, an apt metaphor, or a potential title.

If inspiration strikes, rejoice! Capture those ideas as soon as possible.

The best insights often arrive at the least convenient moments. The Muse can be annoying that way. Be ready with multiple methods for capturing those fleeting thoughts.

- Keep a pen and paper handy
- Record a voice memo in your phone
- Use a note-taking tool like Evernote to make notes from your phone and then access them from your laptop.
- When all else fails, create a mnemonic strategy for remembering your ideas until you can get someplace where you can write them down. Remember key

words that trigger the idea, or think of stories or images to trigger the recollection.

If the "aha!" moment eludes you, that's fine. The nuggets of insight are like icing on the cake; lovely but not essential.

The most important thing is that you have given the Scribe a rest and opened up the topic to the subconscious parts of your mind. When you next sit down with focused attention to write, you'll start from a different place and the process should be smoother and faster.

The insights from incubation may send you back to research different avenues. The path through the writing process isn't always linear.

Chapter 10

Structure the Ideas

The next step before drafting is to map out what you plan to write. Assemble your research notes and develop a structure and concept for the piece you're creating.

In an essay about structure in *The New Yorker*, John McPhee praises a high school teacher who required him to submit three writing assignments per week (yowza), along with a structural outline for each. Writes McPhee, "It could be anything from roman numerals I, II, III to a looping doodle with guiding arrows and stick figures. The idea was to build some form of blueprint before working it out in sentences and paragraphs."[1]

Don't start creating without a blueprint. The result of this step may take any number of forms, including:

- A traditional outline, with hierarchical sections and subsections
- A scribbled page of ideas lined up in the right sequence
- Notecards carefully arranged in order

- A mind map (a visual structure for taking notes and organizing information)
- An Excel spreadsheet—I know one author who referenced a spreadsheet as the outline for a book

For the purposes of this chapter, we'll refer to the structure as an outline.

You might ask, why not jump directly into drafting? Isn't it faster to start composing the piece?

An outline is like a map to unknown destinations; it prevents you from wasting time on digressions. Knowing where you are gives you the ability to plan and manage the work.

During the drafting phase, you may outgrow the outline that you start with. For each book that I have written, the outline has shifted when the first draft was more than halfway complete. Yes, this meant tearing things apart and putting them back together again, and reworking chapters that had already been drafted.

I didn't discover the final outline until the process of drafting exposed the problems with the original approach and suggested a different structure.

The true test of an outline or structure is the act of writing from it.

Step Three: Structure

Who's in Charge

The Scribe

What You Need

- Focused attention
- Notes from the research phase
- Your favorite outlining tools: pen or pencil and paper, word processor, mind-mapping software, notecards and markers, whiteboard, etc.

Steps

1. Clarify your objectives
2. Review your research and notes
3. Create the structure
4. Paste your notes into the outline structure to prime the drafting
5. Share with others (if required)

Clarify Your Objectives

Before undertaking any writing project, clarify your objectives. Specifically, understand the audience, the medium, and the purpose of the piece. When working on collaborative projects, nailing down these objectives early in the process prevents rework later.

Audience: Who is the ideal reader for the piece? What knowledge does this person have already? Identify the broad audience and the profile of the ideal reader.

- A corporate blog post should be written with a specific set of readers in mind, typically customers or prospects. For marketing content, refer to customer personas developed as part of your content marketing strategy.
- A nonfiction book is geared to a specific set of readers likely to buy the book.
- Even fictional works have ideal readers. Stephen King claims that his wife Tabitha is his Ideal Reader.

Stephen King's readership is far beyond the core demographic of his wife. But having a reader in mind helps him in the drafting and revision process. The same will be true for you.

Medium: How will people consume what you're creating? Will it appear in an online blog or a book? Will readers use paper or a digital device? Will there be an audio version?

The final published format affects the outline and structure. If you're planning a lengthy nonfiction book, you'll approach the outline quite differently from a short story or blog post series. Of course, work originating with one concept may shift over time, but you have to start somewhere.

Purpose: Is there an explicit message? An implicit one?

You may have both. This happens in business writing all the time; the explicit purpose of a marketing ebook is providing valuable information for customers. The implicit purpose is demonstrating expertise and gaining trust.

Review Your Notes

With the objectives firmly in mind, read through your notes once more, this time with pen and paper (or your favorite outlining method) at hand. Review your research notes and freewriting files.

Look for trends and possible approaches to the structure.

For a nonfiction piece, list all the things you want to cover and points you intend to make. I like to create an online file containing relevant research I plan to use.

Create the Structure

Sort through everything you want to cover and figure out the best structure to meet the needs of your message, your audience, and your purpose. (Yes, that's a tall order.) Exactly how you do this depends on what works for you.

Some people prefer to put ideas on paper or notecards and scatter them around the workplace. Others create hierarchical outlines, with roman numerals and neatly indented subheads.

Personally, I find technology distracting at this phase. I prefer to grab a piece of paper and start writing down and connecting thoughts and notes. Then I clean it up and consolidate my notes into a concise, comprehensive skeleton of the end result. This eventually becomes an outline in a word processing file.

My friend and prolific writer Roger C. Parker uses mind mapping to connect thoughts with outlying ideas in a visual map. He draws these links first by hand, then uses software to create online mind maps he can share with others.

You know your own brain best, so do what works for you—short of carving the outline in stone.

Avoid committing too strongly to the exact outline. The structure may adapt as you write, particularly for longer works like books.

Prepare the Outline for Drafting

Optionally, populate the outline with notes and thoughts to accelerate the drafting process.

Combine the outline structure you've created with the relevant bits of research or freewriting. If using an electronic file, cut and paste notes into the appropriate sections. If you're a fan of paper or notecards, arrange them in groups so you have the materials sorted and ready to jog your memory as you begin composing each section of the piece.

Sharing Outlines

In business or other collaborative environments, you may need to share the structure with others before starting the first draft. In this case, make a cleaner, condensed version of the outline you plan to work with—a document that will make sense to others.

A clean, presentable outline can help you get feedback, approval, or even funding. For example, book proposals include chapter outlines. A pile of notecards won't cut it.

When collaborating with others, use the outline phase to get everyone to agree with the approach before you start writing. It's much easier to change course at this point than after you've written thousands of words. However, make it clear that the outline is a work in progress, as further exploration may reveal unexpected insights.

---

[1] John McPhee, "Structure: Beyond the Picnic Table Crisis," *New Yorker*, January 14, 2013.

Chapter 11

Write the First Draft

At last you're ready to start transferring ideas and thoughts into a form that you can share with the world. Ideally, the previous steps have prepared you for efficient and effective drafting. Now it's time to get the words out of your head and onto paper.

The drafting phase is neither the start nor the end of the writing process. Don't set your sights on finishing yet.

Begin this phase with two key objectives:

First, get a complete draft down on paper or in a file quickly, even if it is imperfect.

Second, make the process as enjoyable as possible by inviting a state of flow.

Not every author follows this strategy. Some prefer to refine and polish the text as they draft. That may be your preference as well. If you want to experience the state of flow during writing, your best bet may be to draft quickly and revise at leisure.

The drafting phase integrates the discipline and knowledge of the Scribe with the creativity and inspiration of the Muse. Self-criticism inhibits the Muse and detracts from the unified state of flow.

Remember that people operating in a state of flow work without self-consciousness or fear. By drafting quickly, you silence the inner editor and encourage the collaboration of the Scribe and the Muse.

Stephen King speaks of writing the first draft with the door closed (for yourself), and the second with the door open (for others).[1] Ernest Hemingway phrased it this way: "You put down the words in hot blood, like an argument, and correct them when your temper has cooled."[2]

Even if you cannot achieve flow, the drafting phase requires the consistent and alternating contributions of the Scribe and Muse. Editing inhibits the Muse. Try to draft fearlessly and fluidly.

Step Four: Drafting

Who's in Charge

The Scribe and the Muse collaborate (when you realize flow) or contribute in alternating bursts (the rest of the time)

What You Need

- Periods of both focused and open attention
- A distraction-free place to work (your ideal environment for flow)
- Your favorite tools for drafting

Steps

1. Define your objectives
2. Write without self-criticism
3. Rest
4. Revisit and continue

Define Daily or Weekly Objectives

The drafting phase may last a single morning if you're creating something short and simple. It may span days, weeks, or months for a book. Speed often varies by project.

If you enter a state of flow and write for hours without noticing the passage of time, congratulations! More often, you can only focus for a while before the Scribe takes a break, leaving you sitting unproductively at the desk, daydreaming. For projects requiring multiple sessions, set clear objectives: a word count, page count, part of the outline, or amount of focused time. Then commit to achieving them.

If you're working on a long project like a book, define multiple milestones and create a plan for getting through the whole thing.

Many writers don't let themselves leave the desk until they have completed a minimum word or page count. I set objectives based on the project, and do my best work in chunks of time ranging from an hour to 90 minutes. After that, I lose focus. I repeat as many of those chunks as necessary until I reach my objective for the day.

Don't worry about setting down the sections in the order people will read them. Draft those parts of the text that your brain is ready to write. If you've been thinking about a chapter and have thoughts circulating on that topic, work on it. You may end up creating several sections in parallel. Use the revision phase to make sure the whole thing makes sense when assembled in linear order.

Write for Flow

Find a physical environment that is conducive for achieving flow, away from the interruptions of the daily world. Turn off notifications, close other applications, shut the door, silence the phone. Do whatever it takes to create surroundings in which it is possible to lose yourself in work. (Revisit the chapter on flow for thoughts on identifying an ideal environment.) Then start writing.

Remember that during flow, we lose self-consciousness and fear. When creating the first draft, turn off the inner critic and be fearless.

Give yourself permission to use lame verbs or awkward phrases if the thoughts are flowing. Beauty and brilliance emerge during revision. Your first draft won't be the final product, so don't worry about its imperfections.

- If you hate the way a sentence sounds or cannot find the right word, add a notation. My first drafts are filled with highlighted text or comments saying "fix this!"

- If you run into an issue you don't know how to resolve, make a note of it and keep going as if you'd fixed it. You'll refer to it again later.

Not every great author follows this strategy. James Joyce famously took great care with each word, averaging about 90 words per day in the eight years he spent composing *Ulysses*. (Can you imagine being the copyeditor for *Ulysses*?)

You might suppose it would be faster to write a terrific, publishable first draft, rather than revising.

It would be, if you aren't human. But I suspect that you are.

Writing and editing use different neural networks and mental processes. Doing both together requires mental multitasking, which few of us do well.

As you perfect the craft and learn your particular foibles, your first drafts will get better and require less copyediting. But in most cases, the fastest path to a good finished product is to get the words down on paper in the first pass, without stopping to criticize, edit, and correct.

Just write.

Rest

Unless you're creating something short, completing the first draft will take more than one writing session. Between the periods of focus you will go about the rest of your life.

Treat the breaks as mini incubation periods; before you quit a session, make a note about what you plan to work on next. Ask yourself a question or two. If you've been tracking unresolved issues or making notes in the draft, look them over before you stop working.

If good ideas strike when you're away from the work, write them down where you will see them when you next work.

In the book *Process: The Writing Lives of Great Authors*, Sarah Stodola describes how Toni Morrison incubates her ideas as she goes about her life: "She's always thinking about writing while doing other things, washing the dishes or when she was putting her sons to bed, so that when she does find herself in front of a piece of paper, she's ready to put something on it."[3]

Layer the Draft

Getting everything down on paper may require more than one pass through the draft. When creating the first draft quickly, and particularly when working in a state of flow, you may skim over an area in order to keep going, or omit important detail or texture.

Consider taking a second pass through the writing to fill it out. The journalist Donald Murray referred to the practice as *layering*, likening it to adding layers in an oil painting to change the texture and color. As Murray describes it, "The act of layering can be forgiving. We don't have to get it all right today, we just have to do a decent job on one element in the text."[4]

This second, layering pass is not really a revision. Instead, it's a chance to flesh out and complete the content.

In the days before word processors, many authors would write first drafts by hand, then type them up at night or early the next day. During typing, they would rework or add to the original draft. Other authors who composed on the typewriter would retype the pages from the day before, layering the first draft while getting a running start on the next day's work.

Word processors eliminate the need for a separate typing pass. But you can reread and revisit the previous day's work before continuing, easing into the current day's work while adding depth to what is already there.

Repeat Until Done

The drafting phase may be filled with many cycles of incubation and struggle. Remember Csikszentmihalyi's five phases of creativity? The fifth phase, elaboration, goes on for a while, and itself contains iterative cycles of creativity: "This part of the process is constantly interrupted by periods of incubation and is punctuated by small epiphanies."[5]

Eventually, you'll make it to the point at which you have a first draft. It may be terrible, filled with incomplete sentences and notes to yourself, but it's all there.

Congratulations! You're not done, but you've got the foundation to build on. Sometimes it will be pretty darned good, and other times the draft is a mere skeleton of your vision for the piece. To determine which is true, get some distance from the words. That brings us to the next critical step: let it rest.

Resources

For stories about writers' lives and processes, see Sarah Stodola's book *Process: The Writing Lives of Great Authors.*

---

[1] Stephen King, *On Writing: A Memoir of the Craft* (New York: Scribner, 2010) 209–210.

[2] A. E. Hotchner, *Papa Hemingway: A Personal Memoir* (Boston: Da Capo Press, 2005).

[3] Sarah Stodola, *Process: The Writing Lives of Great Authors* (Kindle edition.) (Seattle: Amazon Publishing, 2015), 16.

[4] Donald M. Murray, *Writing to Deadline: The Journalist at Work* (Portsmouth, NH: Heinemann, 2000), 150–151.

[5] Mihaly Csikszentmihalyi, *Creativity: Flow and the Psychology of Discovery and Invention* (New York: HarperPerennial, 1996), 79.

Chapter 12

Let the Draft Rest

After the beating and kneading phase of bread making, both the kneader and the dough have earned a rest. The baker puts the dough aside in a safe place so the unseen yeast organisms will do their magic during the first rise. During this time, home bakers can go off and do other things, knowing that more work lies ahead.

Writing similarly benefits from a period of rest when the first draft is completed. Taking a break gives your brain another opportunity to incubate the concepts in the text. Perhaps more importantly, you need distance to change your perspective on the draft, to switch gears from creator to reviser and editor.

For short works on a tight deadline, this rest period may only last an hour or so. You may want to leave longer projects alone for a week or two. External deadlines often dictate the length of the rest period.

Here, too, writing is like baking bread: "Rising time will vary, since this depends on the temperature of all the ingredients in the dough, the amount of yeast and the kinds of flour and additive used, the temperature of the bowl, altitude, and the place you set the bowl."[1]

The art lies in knowing how long to wait.

Step Five: Let the Draft Rest

Who's in Charge

The Scribe *must* take a break during this phase; the Muse may choose to return

What You Need

- At least one full night of sleep
- Elapsed time

Steps

1. Make a wish list of the problems you'd like to solve.
2. Let time pass.

Make a Wish List

This rest period is an opportunity to put your subconscious brain to work on problems in the draft so far—calling on the Zeigarnick Effect described in the chapter on creativity. Provide a gentle nudge in the right direction by making notes of unresolved issues in the first draft.

- If you have been leaving notes to yourself in the draft or creating lists of unresolved issues, review them now so you remember what to ponder.
- If there's an area you're not happy with, such as the introduction or ending, make a mental note of that.

Inviting inspiration is not the main purpose of this rest period, but it never hurts! If new ideas do appear during the rest period, add them to a list of things to address during revision.

Leave Time

The revision step requires that you look at the first draft with a fresh perspective. Let enough time elapse so you're not wedded to the specific words in the first draft.

Try to let anything sit at least overnight before you start revising, even if it's a short piece. During sleep, and specifically the REM cycle of sleep, your brain is hard at work making connections and processing the activities of the day. Science actually backs up the old advice to "sleep on it."

Time and distance do amazing things. The sections you thought were brilliant may seem clumsy when you see them with fresh eyes. But you may also be surprised by a draft that is better than you imagined. We tend to remember vividly the struggles and forget the parts that went well during the drafting phase.

You can work on other projects, in other phases, while this one rests.

---

[1] Ellen Foscue Johnson, "The Basic Loaf Recipe," *Garden Way Publishing's Bread Book: A Baker's Almanac* (Charlotte, VT: Garden Way Publishing, 1979), 13.

Chapter 13

Revise

Revision is like the second cycle of kneading in the bread-baking process. After you've let the dough rise in a lovingly sheltered location, you attack it again, sometimes with violence. The instructions for my favorite bread recipe are particularly telling: "Give the dough a good sock with your fist. This is called punching the dough down. It will heave a sigh as it collapses…"[1]

Like kneading, revision is where much of the hard work of writing happens. Without revision, we leave the quality of our work to chance, hoping that in the drafting phase, the inspiration was good enough. Through revision and editing, decent prose becomes compelling, entertaining, or beautiful.

You don't always have time for revision beyond a cursory read-through. You might even skip that for an email to your mom, although given the vagaries of auto-correction technologies on smartphones, it's always a good idea to reread before pressing Send.

The more important the quality of the work, the more time you want to dedicate to revision. You may make one revision pass or cycle through the piece several times depending on the length of the text, your own standards, the quality of the first draft, and the timing of the publication.

Approach the revision process from the top down, starting with the broadest perspective and working your way into detail:

- Structural revision: Is everything in the right order? Does the piece hang together?
- Revision for flow: Can the reader make sense of what you're trying to say? Revise for readability and comprehension.
- Copy revision: Look at tone and style, word choice, and grammar.
- Proofreading: Do the words actually appear on paper as you think they do?

It makes no sense to agonize over word choice if you later decide to cut that section or completely rework how you present the material. Likewise, looking for typos and spelling errors is wasted effort if you later reword for reasons of style or clarity. For short pieces, you may be able to combine several of these revisions in one read-through.

Revision is hard work. For projects like a book, the task is too daunting to take on alone; enlist editors for outside perspective and expertise.

This chapter shares multiple strategies for the revising; choose those that meet your preferences and needs.

Step Six: Revise

Who's in Charge

The Scribe runs this phase, ideally with occasional input from the Muse

What You Need

- Focused attention
- The rough draft
- Editing tools (paper, electronic)
- Friends, editors, colleagues
- Patience

Steps

1. Start with structure and work your way down
2. Revise tone and style for reader's flow; look for cultural biases, the fallacy of sounding smart, the Curse of Knowledge, and self-indulgence
3. Edit iteratively
4. Proofread

Enlist outside help for any or all of these steps.

Revise for Structure

Read through the first draft to assess what you've got. It may be better than you think, or it may be worse.

Make sure the structure of the piece works at all levels, from the organization to the headings. Here are a few things to check:

Headings and subheadings: Can the reader navigate the piece? What happens if someone doesn't read it from start to finish, but in bursts? Does the structure make sense?

Premise: Will readers understand what you're doing and why they should invest the time in reading?

Order: Have you chosen an effective way to present the information? Even when narrating a story, you may choose to start with the ending or in the middle.

Repetition or consistency: Does the draft repeat itself? If so, is it intentional and effective? Do concepts appear in the right order?

As you evaluate the structure, you'll notice other things you want to change. You may find that you repeat certain words, or notice an awkward transition. Mark these spots in the manuscript or keep a running list of problems to address. Revision is iterative.

Revise for the Reader's Flow

Up to this point, the writing recipe has focused on optimizing the processes and operation of the writer's brain. The revision process is your chance to streamline processes in the *reader's* brain. Switch the focus from writing to reading.

Do the work now so your reader doesn't have to later.

The first draft is scattered with artifacts of your thought processes. Revision is your opportunity to transfer those ideas into other people's minds. Make the experience of reading as fluid as possible.

The difficulty, of course, is getting the reader's perspective. Read your work aloud to someone else; you will notice where things sound awkward. Ask others to look through the text and make a note anytime they had to double back and reread a sentence. Checking a sentence twice distracts the reader from the meaning.

Look for the following biases and problems:

- Cultural biases
- The fallacy of sounding smart
- The Curse of Knowledge
- Self-indulgence

Cultural Biases in Tone and Style

Every culture has its own tone and style preferences. Especially when writing for an international audience, hunt out your own cultural biases and see if they make sense for the audience.

I once worked on website copy for a technology company founded by engineers from Spain. The founder complained when I pared down the lengthy, flowing sentences into simpler prose that was easier to read and digest on the webpage. He told me that in Spain, educated people wrote in long, complex sentences. He worried that the simpler prose made the founders appear less intelligent. Yet the target audience for the website consisted of impatient Americans, reading online. He had to put aside his instinct for the sake of the audience.

Biases occur within industries and genres as well. Academics, for example, often craft lengthy, grammatically correct sentences that mirror their thought processes through complex subjects. As a student, I remember trying to assume an "academic" tone when writing papers, hoping to impress my professors. Which leads us to the next pitfall: attempting to appear smart.

The Fallacy of Sounding Smart

Writing is a window into the author's thought process, and we all want others to think we're smart. This urge to appear learned may tempt us to use abstruse words, or spin complex sentences instead of simpler constructions.

Adding complexity to your writing does *not* make you seem smarter. You should write in the tone and style that matches your audience's expertise and expectations. Lawyers writing for other lawyers, for example, use their own way of communicating that the layman struggles to understand.

Outside of specific, work-related contexts, most readers can stop at any time if they lose patience and move on to other things.

If you want people to think you're brilliant, communicate intelligent thoughts effectively.

The drive to "sound smart" arises from a misplaced focus. Stop thinking about how the reader sees *you*, the author, and worry about what the reader is experiencing in their own brains. When you worry about sounding intelligent, your focus is on yourself, not the reader.

Perhaps you genuinely think in complex and abstract thoughts, so your first drafts come out that way. If you're communicating with a broader audience that doesn't share your background, use the revision process to simplify and clarify, so that readers can share your insights.

Your thinking voice doesn't have to be your writing voice.

Create the first draft in whatever way works best for you. Craft long, complex sentences filled with passive voice if that keeps you in a state of flow. Then edit those sentences before sending them out into the world.

Readers shouldn't have to travel exactly the same thought processes that you did. Do the work of smoothing the path for them.

The Curse of Knowledge

In economic theory, the Curse of Knowledge describes a pervasive cognitive bias that makes it difficult to imagine or remember the perspective of someone who lacks your current understanding.

We experience this as readers when authors use acronyms without spelling them out first, or buzzwords without definitions.

If you're discussing a technical topic for a nontechnical audience, start by understanding their baseline knowledge.

Your task is to explain the basics clearly, without boring the reader who already has the grounding in the topic. It's a delicate balance.

The deeper your knowledge of an area, the more difficult it is to escape the Curse of Knowledge.

Michael Lewis is a master at avoiding the Curse of Knowledge. In *The Big Short*, he explains the complex mortgage-backed securities at the root of the 2008 market meltdown. In *Flash Boys*, he describes "dark pools" and high-frequency trading strategies, and how stock exchanges are rigged against individual investors. In each book, he explains esoteric topics well enough for the layperson to understand, while entertaining readers of any knowledge level. He does so, in part, by using metaphors and stories.

Revision should target the Curse of Knowledge. As the author, you remember what you meant to say when you wrote the text. You can retrace the thought processes that led to a specific sentence.

The cognitive scientist, linguist, and author Steven Pinker sums up the source of bad writing: "The main cause of incomprehensible prose is the difficulty of imagining what it's like for someone else not to know something that you know."[2]

We know how our brains got to the point of what we're saying. We may not realize that other people's brains, not starting in the same place, aren't coming along with us.

The best defense against the Curse of Knowledge during the revision process is to solicit outside opinions. Hire an editor, or ask friends and colleagues for honest feedback. Make sure they understand the expected reader for the piece.

Self-Indulgence

The revision process is our last, best chance to integrate the reader's perspective. Otherwise, we risk the sin of self-indulgence: writing for our own needs, without regard for the audience.

When practicing freewriting, you record the voices and thoughts rocketing around in your head. If you are in a state of flow while drafting, you may continue to follow those internal voices that keep the words moving. During revision, ask yourself a critical question: Is this useful to my ideal reader, or am I writing entirely to please myself? Is this self-indulgent?

Self-indulgence is a matter of perspective.

As a high school student reading William Faulkner's stream of consciousness, or a college student wading through James Joyce's *Ulysses*, I felt that the authors indulged a tendency to push boundaries of grammar and patience. Returning to these works in later years, I no longer hold that view. More likely, those authors had a specific ideal reader in mind—one who was *not* trying to plough through novels as quickly as possible so she could do something fun that evening and still be prepared for class the next day. I was nowhere near the ideal reader for those novels.

Yet even when I am legitimately a member of the target audience for a text, I frequently encounter writing that seems self-indulgent. The author hasn't taken the time to account for my presence by trimming unnecessary words or digressions.

In her book *Everybody Writes*, Ann Handley explains it perfectly: "Good writing serves the reader, not the writer. It isn't self-indulgent. Good writing anticipates the questions that readers might have as they're reading a piece, and it answers them."[3]

Writing about yourself is an effective way to get the ink flowing. Unless you're publishing a journal, take the reader's perspective during revision.

Edit, then Edit, then Edit

Just as we have unique fingerprints, authors have personal ticks and idiosyncrasies that litter first drafts. These may include grammatical mistakes, spelling problems, or awkward phrasing. You may exhibit an obsession with ellipses...

(See what I did there?)

...or parenthetical comments. I suffer from both of those problems.

It's not worth sacrificing the state of flow to correct these idiosyncrasies as you draft.

Many of these issues are simply artifacts of the way you think. That quirky sentence construction may reflect a creative, circuitous thought process. Don't try to edit those thoughts as you're drafting. Inviting the inner editor to the drafting process will inhibit creativity and may slow you down.

Instead, learn your personal quirks and use them as entry points for revision.

As with many things in life, the first step is acknowledging your problems. Make a list of them. Others can detect your writing weaknesses with much more ease than you can—our own faults are surprisingly elusive. Ask a knowledgeable editor to look for recurring trends and problems in draft.

Hiring a skilled editor to go through your work is one of the best investments you can make in your long-term writing career. Use the edit not only to fix the current piece, but also to identify trends and problems in your prose for the future.

If you cannot hire an editor, ask a knowledgeable friend to be brutally honest. Tell him or her that you're looking for your unique quirks.

For example:

- Do you repeat the same word several times in a paragraph?
- Do you rely on the passive voice?
- Suffer from dangling participles, sentence fragments, or parallel construction issues?[4]

Behind each marked edit or revision, look for stylistic or habitual trends. Make a list of the top four or five issues in your writing. You probably won't be able to fix everything, so choose only a few candidates.

Make these your first targets during revision. If you've written the first draft without self-criticism, then these flaws will be there, large as life, in your draft copy. Use them to jump-start the revision.

For the sake of illustration, I'll share a few of my own weaknesses with you. I'm not proud of them, but they're mine.

When writing in a state of flow, I rely heavily on the variations of the verb "to be." Mary Norris made me feel better by reporting, in her book *Between You and Me*, that "to be" is a *copulative* verb. But the suggestive label doesn't make those verbs any more exciting in the prose.

Also, when I'm in the drafting groove, I use adjectives like "big" and "new" a lot. And "a lot." I use that a lot, too. In revision, I'll hunt out those words and replace them with better alternatives.

My revision hit list also includes waffling words that weaken my points, such as:

- Some
- Perhaps
- Should
- Certain
- Very

I do a global search for each of those words and start examining and reworking sentences when I find them. These easy entry points bring me into the draft from a different perspective; I rework those areas to streamline the reader's comprehension or amp up the prose.

If you follow this process, your quirks will evolve over time. After several revision cycles, you will internalize corrections to easy-to-fix mistakes and they'll stop appearing in drafts. Drop them from your list; you can always find other idiosyncrasies to replace them.

Your intended tone and style determines whether a writing mannerism is appropriate for the audience and medium. Textbooks are often impersonal; personal blogs may support the informal tone and style, letting you trail off with ellipses...

Understand how the mannerisms affect the tone and style. Make the intentional decision to either accept or rephrase them, rather than leaving them in place in ignorance.

Keep going through your list, revising and editing until one or more of the following conditions are met:

- You're sufficiently satisfied with the result.
- You run out of time.
- You cannot stand to look at the piece ever again.

Eventually you reach a point of diminishing returns. Often the outside world intervenes.

Nora Ephron describes the process of revising and finalizing a screenplay as follows: "The moment you stop work on a script seems to be determined not by whether you think the draft is good but simply by whether shooting is about to begin: if it is, you get to call your script a final draft; and if it's not, you can always write another revision. This might seem to be a hateful way to live, but the odd thing is that it's somehow comforting; as long as you're revising, the project isn't dead."[5]

Proofread

Before you put bread in the oven to bake, you let the shaped loaves rise one more time in a process called "proofing." (I'm not kidding—how perfect is that as a metaphor?) In writing, the proofreading phase is too important to skip.

Proofreading is your final chance to fix errors and mistakes. Examine the piece in its final format so you can find awkward line breaks or unintended consequences of the layout.

How you approach the proofreading stage depends on timing and resources.

- Hire a proofreader.
- Act like Guy Kawasaki and use crowdsourcing, asking multitudes of volunteers. (This strategy works well if you have an enormous social media following.)
- Check your own work, reading it aloud or backward to interrupt the part of your brain that already knows what it says.
- Ask friends and colleagues to look for errors.

In the best possible world, you would do as many of these as possible: proofread yourself, ask others, *and* hire a professional. No one will catch everything.

Even if you're a meticulous proofreader—the type of person who looks through phone bills for typos—you have a significant handicap when checking your own writing. Because part of you "knows" what the text *should* say, you'll look right past problems like repeated or missing words. It's the Curse of Knowledge all over again, on a smaller scale. We see what we think is there, not what's really there.

To get around the Curse of Knowledge at this final stage of revision, have someone else proofread the work. If you cannot afford to hire a proofreader, consider trading the service with another writer. Offer to proofread each others' pieces. Decide on the style guide for your piece. If in doubt, ask the proofreader to observe the AP Style Guide, and provide any specialized terminology or abbreviations that you plan to use.

If you must proof your own work, consider using these strategies:

Let time elapse. Wait at least overnight before you proofread. As time passes, your memory of the exact details of every sentence will fade, so you can see what's truly there on the paper.

Read out loud. If you're planning to create an audiobook, consider recording it when you're in the final proofreading stage. You'll be amazed at how much you find.

Read the text backward. Start with the last sentence, then the one before, etc. This disrupts the narrative flow in your head, enabling you to see issues like stray or missing words.

Don't rely on technology alone. Spell checking and grammar checking are necessary, but not sufficient. Spell checkers don't catch certain categories of mistakes, such as missing words or the wrong word that's spelled correctly. And Microsoft's grammar checker is easily confounded by complex sentences. However, a sentence that confuses the grammar checker may also trip up the casual reader. Review any highlighted areas to spot sentences that need rewording.

Strategies for Mitigating the Curse of Knowledge

- **Best**: Get other opinions. Ask someone else to read the piece. Hire an editor.
- **OK**: Create distance through time. Wait hours or overnight between revision passes or proofreading.
- **In a crunch**: Change your location. Read the text aloud. Do whatever you can to change your perspective on the text. Don't sit in the same place

where you wrote the piece. Walk around with a printed copy or change the online view or screen size.

Outside Edits and Opinions

You can enlist external editors for each stage of the revision cycle. Developmental editors look at structure, line editors focus on flow and consistency, copyeditors dive into grammar and punctuation, and proofreaders scrutinize the final copy.

You may turn to outside assistance at any or all of these phases, either hiring editors, running the piece by experts, or asking trusted friends and advisors.

When engaging outside editors or experts:

- Understand and communicate the type of editing you seek. Do you want developmental editing, which is welcome earlier in the process, or copyediting later on? Proofreading?

- Share the ideal reader, purpose, and attempted tone and style with the editor. The more the editor understands about what you're trying to do, the better advice they can provide.

Authors sometimes maintain awkward relationships with editors. A few argue or wrestle with comments from others. This may be a symptom of the *self-serving bias*—the tendency to overlook our own failures and reject criticism.

While writers need self-confidence, everyone benefits from the ability to recognize and correct problems. An expert editor is the writer's most valuable friend, offering essential defenses against the Curse of Knowledge and self-indulgence.

The challenge, of course, lies in finding the right editor.

When engaging someone for developmental editing, make sure the person knows and understands your target audience and the purpose of the piece, which you identified in the outlining/structural phase of the writing process. If there's a creative brief, share it with the editor.

Even the most brilliant consultants or editors may give poor advice if they do not agree with the main objectives of the piece. As the author, you know what you are trying to do and must be prepared to defend it.

Line editors must understand your tone and style. Ann Handley suggests that "great line editors are hard to find. If you find one, hold on to him or her; get married, if you must."[6]

Find people who have worked on pieces similar to yours or with authors you trust. If necessary, start with a small project to see how the two of you work together. Build relationships with the editors you admire and respect.

Resources

During a prolonged revision process, it helps to draw strength from others. I love Steven Pinker's *The Sense of Style,* and suggest that you look at this book early in the revision process, when you can act on its inspiration. Ann Handley's *Everybody Writes: Your Go-To Guide to Creating Ridiculously Good Content* offers terrific guidance on revising, particularly in the business context.

For a peek inside the mental workings of an expert and passionate copyeditor, read *Between You and Me: Confessions of a Comma Queen* by Mary Norris, who has spent three decades at *The New Yorker*, copyediting everything from works of literary greats to Christmas shopping lists. The book is a window into her particular view on the world of letters, and will give you a better appreciation of the copyeditor's burdens and joys.

---

[1] Ellen Foscue Johnson, *Garden Way Publishing's Bread Book: A Baker's Almanac*, (Charlotte, VT: Garden Way Publishing, 1979), 14.

[2] Steven Pinker, *The Sense of Style: The Thinking Person's Guide to Writing in the 21st Century* (New York: Viking, 2014), 57.

[3] Ann Handley, *Everybody Writes: Your Go-To Guide to Creating Ridiculously Good Content* (Hoboken, NJ: Wiley, 2014), 44.

[4] Bonus copyediting point to anyone who chafed at the inconsistency of structure in this bullet list!

[5] Nora Ephron, "Revision and Life: Take it From the Top—Again," originally published in the *New York Times*, November 9, 1986.

[6] Ann Handley, *Everybody Writes*, 78.

Chapter 14

Publish When Ready

Whether it entails pushing a button or firing up the printing presses, publishing would seem to fall outside of the writing process.

Deciding to publish is a critical, final phase of writing. By treating it as a distinct step in the process, you can schedule it to leave a pocket of time between revision and publication.

Often the publication decision isn't entirely in your hands—external forces decide for you. If you have a deadline, try to finish revising at least the night before, so you can give your brain a quick rest and take one more look before publishing.

Let the work sit overnight before publishing.

The rest of this chapter is for those situations in which you must decide precisely when to stop revising and release the work into the world.

The baker's final challenge is choosing the right moment to remove the loaf from the oven. My favorite baking recipe describes the moment of judgment as follows: "Give the bottom a tap with one fingernail. If it produces a hollow sound, it is done. Try this a few times and you will learn to distinguish the dull thud of an undone loaf from the hollow thump of a done one."[1]

Where the eyes may deceive, the ear offers guidance.

Similarly, you'll have to sense when it's time to let go of your writing. Will it land with a dull thud in front of your readers, or will it resonate? Can you manage another revision, or have you reached a stage of diminishing returns, when impatience to get the work out into the world finally wins? Timing varies in every situation.

When publishing, balance patience and
impatience to serve the readers.

Step Seven: Publishing

Who's in Charge

The Scribe

What You Need

- A deadline (external or internal)
- Patience to get it right
- Impatience to get the words into the world

Steps

1. Let the draft sit at least overnight.
2. Decide to publish.

Patience and Impatience

The process of preparing a work for publication may take longer than anticipated, with time spent:

- Waiting for revisions or proofreading
- Checking facts or getting permission to use content
- Seeking input from others who care deeply or have important insight
- Revising iteratively to reach the point at which you like the prose

When the delays are beyond your control, summon the patience to wait them out. Remember, readers do not know or care how many false starts a project had. They see only the text as it appears to them, without knowing its backstory.

When the delays come from within you, at some point you must listen to the voice of impatience. Tell the Scribe to take a break and move on. (Try distracting the Scribe with a different, juicy project to work on instead.)

The cruel reality is that your manuscript, report, or blog post, will never be perfect. There's *always* room to improve.

If you wait for perfection, nothing will ever
be published.

Choose the right moment to say, "This is good enough," and let your words out into the world. Be patient at the start of the revision process and impatient by the end. At a certain point, impatience wins.

---

[1] Ellen Foscue Johnson, *Garden Way Publishing's Bread Book: A Baker's Almanac* (Charlotte, VT: Garden Way Publishing, 1979), 15.

Chapter 15

Scheduling Work

Poor time management can derail the best writers. Having a clear idea of the overall process, you are less likely to run out of time for a critical phase. The seven-step process proves its worth when used to schedule work.

The overview for each of the seven steps suggested which inner personality took the reins: the Muse or the Scribe. As a project travels from research through incubation and drafting, the Muse and the Scribe hand off the work in phases. I like to picture them as soccer teammates, passing a ball back and forth as they cross the field. The better the passing game, the more successful the team. Practice and plan the handoffs between different stages.

When you understand who is in charge at each point, you can schedule multiple projects, lining up the work and environment for the Muse or the Scribe. To revisit important points from Part One:

- The intuitive, inspirational Muse is easily distracted. The best way to access the Muse is to enter a period of open, mind-wandering attention.

- The Scribe is disciplined and intentional, doing its best work with focused attention.

By now, you should have identified ideal environments for focused attention versus open, wandering attention.

Use the seven steps to select your surroundings for the demands of the work. For example, when researching or revising, find a place where the Scribe can focus. When incubating ideas or solving problems, step away from this setting for a change of venue.

Because the drafting phase is most productive and efficient when the Muse and the Scribe collaborate in a state of flow, find uninterrupted slots of time to do this type of work.

Scheduling a Project From Finish to Start

Begin with a deadline. If there's no external due date for the project, make one up. Remember the research on self-discipline: without deadlines, most of us will procrastinate.

Once you have the ending date, work backward through the seven steps to set up interim deadlines. Leave adequate time for incubation and rest between key phases.

For example, assume that you have a 3,000-word article due on the 15th. From experience, you know that you can write 750 words per hour in the drafting phase, when adequately prepared.

Sketch out a schedule in reverse, allocating your work over a manageable two-week period.

14th: Send the article to the publisher (leaving one extra day for catastrophe)

13th: Final proofreading

11th: Send the revised article to a colleague for revision/comments (due back 12th)

10th–11th: Revise the article

7th–8th: Write the first draft (two hours each day is sufficient)

6th: Outline the article

1st–4th: Research: conduct interviews, read, and freewrite

This plan leaves time for incubation between phases and during the drafting phase. Don't delay the research. Give your brain time to start working with the material, even if you don't plan to write anything for a week.

The length of the project will determine the scheduling:

- Longer projects have less well-defined boundaries, with research continuing even as you outline and draft.

- For shorter projects, you might condense the research and outline steps, and draft later the same day. If possible, try to let some time elapse between completing the revision and publishing so that you can spot problems.

Juggling Multiple Projects

After mastering the seven-step process, you can manage several projects concurrently, without burning out or falling behind.

You don't want multiple projects going through the seven steps at exactly the same time. Remember those college students who waited to start their research papers until they were all due; suddenly they had to research three papers, then outline and write three papers. My head hurts simply thinking about it.

Instead, stagger the start times so the projects are in different phases: research, drafting, incubation, revision. Create the right work environment and conditions for each type of work. If you are freshest mentally in the morning, do the drafting first thing. Schedule research and revision for other parts of the day, and remember to leave unstructured time to ponder what you're learning in the research.

The Scribe is most productive while working on one thing at a time. If you have multiple projects in phases requiring the Scribe, such as research, drafting, and revision, dedicate chunks of time to each.

When your projects are staggered and distributed across multiple phases, you can choose the work that best fits your mood. If you are not feeling rested or creative, you might set aside a few hours for research. If you cannot achieve a state of flow while on a plane or in a hotel room, then move on to revision or research.

Having multiple concurrent projects can spur creativity if the topic or subject areas are varied, by inviting cross-pollination of ideas and associations.

When working for multiple clients across different technology sectors, I often found that ideas in one industry resonated with projects in another. An analogy from the healthcare industry was useful when writing for the security sector, for example.

If you manage the scheduling, juggling multiple projects enhances creativity without damaging productivity.

Part Three:
Writers in the World

I wish I could tell you that when you find a perfect process that aligns with the way your brain works, everything goes smoothly from that point on. But as I mentioned already, I don't write fiction.

The real world tends to scoff at the best laid plans. The roof starts leaking. You sprain your ankle. Partway through the first draft, your book idea suddenly seems trite and unmarketable.

An infinite variety of obstacles can interfere with your work. Some are imposed by the outside world, others arise from within. They include:

- Time pressures
- Writer's block
- Negative feedback
- Internal doubts
- External stresses and problems

If you're committed to writing as a major part of your life, you *will* experience most or all of these situations. At times you may feel like you're playing whack-a-mole with them; just as you get past one, another pops up.

Think of the chapters in this section as a troubleshooting guide; when things go wrong or you stall, look here for suggestions on resetting your mind's gears for these situations. Because when we learn to work with our brains, writing can be fun and rewarding.

Chapter 16

Finding Time

Unless you write as a day job, you'll face time challenges. "Not enough time" could be carved on the gravestones of many aspiring authors.

Sometimes people opt to wait for an ideal time: retirement, or some future date when they have saved enough money to leave the office and write a book. They postpone the work for "someday" when the project will fit easily into their lives. And that day may never arrive.

"Someday" writers pass up the chance to hone their skills so they'll be ready when time opens up. They miss the opportunity to grow and learn through writing.

Each of us has the same number of hours in the day; we differ in how we spend those hours.

If writing is your long-term objective, you owe it to yourself to find time, even if it means amassing many small bits of prose or putting off other things. The world always presents more urgent tasks to do. As author and self-proclaimed Essentialist Greg McKeown puts it, "If you don't prioritize your life, someone else will."[1]

Some authors rise in the early morning hours to write. If that works for you, great. Just be careful not to wake me up while you're working.

Up to this point of the book, we have examined ways to make your work more productive. If you understand the cognitive science principles in Part One, you know about the contributions of your different selves to the work. By dividing the writing process into steps, you can get the brain in gear for the work at hand.

However, you still have to find and set aside the minutes or hours to work. If getting up at 5 a.m. isn't your thing, look through these other approaches for making the most of your time.

Find slices of time and solitude. Early in my career, I worked as a product marketing manager at a database backup start-up. Among other things, I was responsible for creating white papers and sales collateral for the company's products.

Interruptions were part of the job. We shared offices and people were always stopping by to ask questions, which made it difficult to do the focused work of creating first drafts.

But when my children stayed home sick from school, I worked from my house, without the buzz of office conversation and requests. Suddenly I could write the longer papers. My kids' colds helped me be more productive, at least when it came to writing white papers.

Was I interrupted at home? Of course. But I found predictable slivers of time to work without interruption and seized them: the length of a nap or the running time of *The*

Little Mermaid. Parents of preschoolers understand how to make the most of small slices of peace.

Examine your day for moments of solitude that you can reclaim for writing; a ride on the train to work, or a quiet early morning reading the paper.

According to researchers at Nielsen, adults in the U.S. spend 31 hours a week watching television, in both live and recorded formats.[2] That number sounds really high. If you are a regular viewer, consider reclaiming one sitcom's worth of time a night.

Reallocate time slots for writing. Until you can experience days of uninterrupted work in a retreat-like setting, they will have to do. Put the Muse and Scribe to work and you can achieve something meaningful, even in small bursts.

Avoid interruptions and temptations. How much time do you spend on the Internet when you are theoretically working?

In a study of online habits in the U.S. by Pew Research, 21 percent of respondents report being online "almost constantly."[3]

When composing and drafting, you have to shut out other distractions—even those that seem urgent. With its constant stream of updates and news, social media taps into a latent Fear of Missing Out (FoMO), or the thought that people are doing or saying something that you should not miss.

If you prioritize what's happening *outside* yourself, you'll never make progress on your personal goals.

You don't have to give up social interactions, streaming videos, Facebook, online games, or watching movies.

Prioritize them instead. Use them as rewards for achieving your writing objectives.

Treat yourself as a client. We often put our own needs or wishes last, behind those of other people. This apparent selflessness may mask uncertainty; we're not sure that committing time to writing makes any sense, so it's the first thing to fall off the schedule.

Architect and author Sarah Susanka wrote *The Not So Big House* while running a thriving architecture practice. It was her first book, and eventually reshaped her career. As she tells the story in an interview with Roger C. Parker, she made it happen by allocating time on her work calendar. She dedicated regular two-hour slots in her schedule, during which she retreated to her home office and worked on her book.

Treat writing as part of your core responsibilities, whether or not it appears in your job description. Consider the commitment to the work as you would an obligation to others. You would not blow off a client meeting to grab coffee with friends, would you? Show up to write with that same dedication.

Save ideas for later. If you truly don't have a spare moment, become a collector of ideas. Keep notebooks, jot down thoughts, and get your brain processing concepts for future projects. When you do finally clear a moment of time, you'll be ready to get to work.

Resources

For advice on paring down activities so you can do the important things, see *Essentialism: The Disciplined Pursuit of Less* by Greg McKeown. The book dedicates an entire chapter to saying no.

---

[1] Greg McKeown, Essentialism: The Disciplined Pursuit of Less (New York: Crown Business, 2014), 10.

[2] The Nielsen Company, "The Total Audience Report Q4 2015," available at http://www.nielsen.com/us/en/insights/reports/2016/the-total-audience-report-q4-2015.html.

[3] Andrew Perrin, "One-Fifth of Americans Report Going Online Almost Constantly," Pew Research Center Fact Tank, December 8, 2015, available at http://www.pewresearch.org/fact-tank/2015/12/08/one-fifth-of-americans-report-going-online-almost-constantly/

Chapter 17

Working Through Writer's Block

Any discussion of obstacles must address the most famous one of all: writer's block.

A few authors insist that the phrase is an excuse for laziness. Others confess to struggling with it, even to walking away from their careers for years at a time.

But what do we mean by the term *writer's block*? Does it refer to those moments when you have nothing to write about? How about having a topic but not knowing how to start? Being stuck in the middle of a draft?

When we apply basic cognitive science and the seven steps of writing to these problems, we might be able to dig down to underlying causes. Here are a few suggestions for dealing with assorted variations of writer's block.

Generating Ideas

If you have nothing to write about or feel depleted of ideas, try the following:

Collect ideas. This is the same strategy that you apply when you have no time: become a collector of ideas. Read and observe. Take notes everywhere you go. Gather thoughts in a journal—not a pour-your-heart-out journal, but a collection of ideas, paragraphs, scenes, and snippets. In his book *Where Good Ideas Come From*, Steven Johnson describes how Charles Darwin maintained a "commonplace" journal, a collection of observations and ideas in which he developed the thoughts that later led him to *On the Origin of Species*.

Write anyway. If you're drawing a blank or stuck, use freewriting to explore topics you want to learn more about.

Acute writer's block may be a case of the inner editor nixing every idea before the Scribe can evaluate and develop them. Use freewriting to shut down that critic and dig deeper for ideas and associations. When you approach the task with a growth mindset, the act of pulling words out of your head may inspire the Muse to contribute ideas.

Filling the Empty Page

Can't get started on a piece? Facing the empty screen or blank page with a sense of terror?

Follow the seven-step process. The blank page fills some people with dread and stops them in their tracks. This fear may be a signal that you're trying to start at step four, assembling the first draft, without gathering the ingredients in research or planning the structure. Your brain isn't ready to work on it yet.

Revisit the first three steps of the process: research, incubation, and outlining/structuring. These steps prime the Scribe and Muse to collaborate on the draft.

Start drafting in the middle. The drafting process doesn't have to follow the linear order of the final result. Many authors only write the introduction once they are well into the development of a piece, when they know how it has unfolded. Start working where you feel confident or have ideas, and skip ahead or backward as needed.

Getting Unstuck

If you're feeling stuck at a particular point or drawing a blank, consider the following:

Invite open attention. Walk the dog, hop in the shower, or snooze for 20 minutes. Do something that doesn't require mental focus, so your mind can drift, inviting the mental systems of the Muse to look for connections or solutions.

Sleep on it. Your brain may provide connections overnight that make the work easier the next day.

Change your environment. If you don't have time to take a walk or wait overnight, try shifting location. Step away from the desk and bring a notebook with you instead of a laptop. Change settings to loosen connections in the brain. The Scribe temporarily retreats and the Muse has a chance to pitch in.

Chapter 18

Taking Negative Feedback in Stride

You're standing on top of a mountain after a long, grueling hike. In the distant west, you spot a looming thundercloud, with a distinctive anvil shape rising high into the atmosphere. After watching for a few moments, you sense that it's heading your way. You could stay and soak up the dramatic panorama, but you clearly remember a story of a hiker being struck by lightning atop a mountain in exactly this situation. Your joy in the view dims, and you head back down the trail and off the exposed peak.

This is a healthy example of the *negativity bias*: our brains react to negative stimuli more quickly and completely than to positive stimuli. As the thunderstorm story illustrates, that inclination serves people well. Over millennia, the strong pull of possible negative outcomes has contributed to the species' long-term survival.

But overweighting the negative can slow you down in the 21st century, which is filled with Internet trolls, online reviews, and social media diatribes. Even the casual comment from an acquaintance—"Why would you write a book on *that* subject?"—can trigger a descent into negative rumination.

If a colleague tells you three things he loved about your blog post and one thing he disliked, which will you remember? The negative one. This bias can prevent you from hearing and absorbing positive comments, coloring your perceptions. Overreacting to the negative may also filter out the learning opportunities within constructive criticism.

In the worst case, we might use the criticism as an excuse to stop when the writing is difficult, rather than continuing to learn.

The negativity bias is an obstacle to growth.

People with a growth mindset treat all feedback as an opportunity to learn. If you react strongly to the negative, it's more difficult to face criticism. And when you dwell on the downside, you will be less willing to take risks and grow.

You can plan ahead of time to counteract the negativity bias. Knowing your mind's patterns is the first step in resisting the pull of the Dark Side.

Plan ahead and stockpile the positive. When a reader gives you a meaningful compliment, record it. File those comments away for the uncertain future.

When your motivation flags or you lose courage, read through the file of positive comments. As you do so, focus on the person who made the comment and the work that inspired it. Say to yourself: *This person found what I did valuable; I should continue and build on it.*

Spin the negative. I once worked for a global software company, compiling a weekly list of market news and analyst opinions for the employees around the world. Along with the market updates, I drafted "talking points" that staff could use when speaking with customers about events.

Occasionally, the stories seemed like potential bad news, such as the launch of a competitive product or an acquisition that threatened the company's market share. In these cases, my go-to marketing response was that the event confirmed the market's viability. For example: "Microsoft's entry into this space validates the widget market—and we're the leader in widgets."

You can put a marketing spin around almost anything, but the best spin revolves around a core truth. Apply a similar strategy to negative comments. For example:

- The criticism is an indication that your work is finding an audience. If you don't hear any negative feedback, no one may be reading what you publish.

- Your words inspired someone to comment, even in the negative. To paraphrase Guy Kawasaki speaking of social media, if you're not pissing someone off, you're not doing it right.

Think like a statistician. Envision a bell curve of potential readers, with the x-axis representing the degree to which people like the work and the y-axis indicating the number of readers. A small percentage of people will hate it, no matter what. They represent the far left of the curve. Others won't particularly care. Many will like it (ideally the bulk of the curve) and a few will love it. It's a numbers game. As long as the number of haters remain a small fringe at the left of the curve, you're fine.

Learn from the critics, but serve the fans. Putting aside the nasty online trolls, do your critics have legitimate points? If you can make yourself read negative reviews, you may gain insight for the future. At the same time, don't lose focus on your ideal reader or target audience; continue to write for them.

Chapter 19

Unmasking the Imposter Syndrome

"I'm not a writer. I've been fooling myself and other people. I wish I were."

John Steinbeck penned these words in the midst of writing *The Grapes of Wrath*, which would win the 1940 Pulitzer Prize and become part of the American literary canon.[1]

That book's success remained in his future in August of 1938 when he wrote that despairing journal entry. However, Steinbeck was not an undiscovered talent at that point. Both *Of Mice and Men* and *Tortilla Flat* had been published to great acclaim. The staged production of *Of Mice and Men* had completed a successful Broadway run, and Steinbeck was in discussions with filmmaker Pare Lorentz about making a film of his novel *In Dubious Battle*. The world considered Steinbeck a legitimate and successful author.

Yet he had at least momentary pangs of that most insidious affliction, the Imposter Syndrome.

Despite its clinical name, the Imposter Syndrome is often a fleeting frame of mind rather than a pervasive condition. It happens when accomplished individuals cannot internalize their own abilities. As demonstrated by Steinbeck, writers are susceptible.

Your own variation on the Imposter Syndrome may follow any number of different scripts:

Who am I to write a book on this topic?

I'm not really an author.

Someone else already said it; I've got nothing worth adding.

During times of difficulty, these thoughts might tempt you to abandon your work at the moment you most need perseverance.

Steinbeck was well past the halfway point of *The Grapes of Wrath*, heading into the home stretch. Yet, there it was: the thought that he was not a writer after all. He didn't let it stop him.

You shouldn't, either.

Welcome doubt as part of the dues you pay. Many people experience the Imposter Syndrome: authors, artists, entrepreneurs, or anyone undertaking a risky endeavor. It doesn't disappear once you find success; it may become more pronounced as the world recognizes your efforts. Acknowledge the feeling without giving in to it. You're in good company—now keep going.

In his wonderful book *Shut Your Monkey*, Danny Gregory suggests that to some extent, having an inner critic is healthy:

"The only people who don't have monkeys camping out in their heads are sociopaths."[2] Take comfort in that thought when the Imposter Syndrome rears its head. You're not a sociopath.

Let actions speak louder than words. Write your 1,000 words, or two pages, or whatever your daily practice is. Let your behavior be your defense.

A writer is a person who writes, so put the Scribe to work. At some point, the doubting voices in your brain must recognize that, by your actions, you're a writer.

This was Steinbeck's solution. Take comfort in the way he concludes the same journal entry in which he declares he is not a writer:

"I'll try to go on with work now. Just a stint every day does it. I keep forgetting."[3]

Resources

For a deeper dive into the Imposter Syndrome, consider *The Secret Thoughts of Successful Women: Why Capable People Suffer from the Imposter Syndrome and How to Thrive in Spite of It* by Valerie Young.

For an irreverent look at the inner critic, read Danny Gregory's *Shut Your Monkey: How to Control Your Inner Critic and Get More Done.*

John Steinbeck's journals during the time he wrote *The Grapes of Wrath* serve as fascinating reading themselves. You hear the voice of the author, pleading with himself to stay on track, agonizing over setbacks, and plotting the path to completion.

It makes compelling reading, as edited by Robert DeMott and compiled in the book *Working Days*, from which I have quoted throughout this book.

---

[1] Robert DeMott, ed., *Working Days: The Journals of The Grapes of Wrath* (New York: Viking Books, 1989), 56.

[2] Danny Gregory, *Shut Your Monkey: How to Control Your Inner Critic and Get More Done* (Cincinnati, HOW Books, 2016), 25.

[3] Ibid.

Chapter 20

Developing Resilience

You *will* have bad days, when the work does not go well. When you cannot come up with a single decent idea or turn of phrase. When the interruptions rain down more heavily than an El Niño downpour.

These days happen to everyone. During the months in which he drafted *The Grapes of Wrath*, Steinbeck bought property, started construction on a house, and sold the house in which he was living and working. He also dealt with his wife's illness, his publisher's pending bankruptcy, visitors, the pounding of hammers from his neighbor's construction project, and a host of days in which he reported feeling awful. Yet he kept at the task.

Use the following ideas when the outside world stacks up against you.

Keep going, especially when it's tough. You may remember this trick from your childhood: stand with your arms at your sides and your right arm against the wall. Now press that arm straight up and out, as if the wall wasn't there. Press hard—the wall's not going anywhere. Count to 30, then relax the arm and step away from the wall.

Your right arm now seems to float up effortlessly. This passed for magic when I was young. But it's muscle memory. When the obstacle is gone, your muscles keep contracting, without conscious effort.

Similarly, writing on the bad days strengthens your mental muscle memory. It may feel like you're straining against an immovable object, but eventually something shifts. When the obstacles disappear, the words will come much more easily.

You've trained your brain to keep going, and that pays off.

Dial back to the daily practice. If you have to abandon your work for a while, keep the daily practice going. Do 750 words a day of freewriting if that's all you have time for. A daily writing practice develops resilience.

Bad writing days and setbacks are opportunities to develop persistence.

If you can't keep going, forgive yourself. If you are unable to write for a while, go back to taking notes or scribbling down ideas when they strike, and restart when you can.

Chapter 21

Finishing a Book

Writing a book is like running a marathon; the experience tests your endurance, and while it happens, you may feel like it will never end. From a cognitive science perspective, completing a book presents at least two serious challenges.

Uncertainty: No one can tell you exactly how the book will turn out or what kind of reception it will find. Uncertainty and ambiguity often make us uncomfortable.

Delayed gratification: Even completing a first draft can take months; getting the book through the publication process can feel like raising a child. The longer you have to wait, the more difficult it becomes to resist the temptation of doing other things. Your future self, the one who has already published the book, seems far away.

This chapter specifically addresses the mental processes of writing a book; publishing and marketing are beyond the scope of this discussion. I'll also restrain myself to a discussion of nonfiction, as that's where my experience lies.

Completing a book requires a huge investment of time, effort, and mental dedication. The payoff—people reading and finding value in the book—is a distant uncertainty. Writing a book inherently requires a leap of faith, and faith has a way of faltering. If you anticipate the temptations, like those children in Walter Mischel's marshmallow studies, you have a fighting chance of resisting them.

The seven-step writing process can help you weather the experience by creating a road map of both the larger process (the book itself) and the individual sections therein. Having a process gives welcome structure to the protracted, uncertain effort of writing the book. By understanding the steps and milestones within the overall objective, you can commit to interim deadlines for yourself while building in feedback on your progress.

The writing process works on two levels for books: at the macro level, tracking the entire book itself, and on a micro level, applied to individual chapters and sections as you work through the book.

- On the macro level, publishing a book is a linear process. As an author, you proceed from idea to outline to draft, through revisions and publication. Simple enough. The seven steps of the process apply at this book-wide level rather well, with minor variations described below.

- From deep within the work, at the micro level, assembling the book's draft doesn't feel neat and orderly. You may shepherd each section or chapter of the book through the steps individually, then assemble the parts into a complete book.

The Seven Steps Applied to a Book

As the book progresses through its path to publication, the seven steps apply with minor modifications.

Step one: Research. The research phase can extend for months or years of discovery and exploration, with incubation embedded in the process. Eventually, the day arrives when you have enough content to move to creating the book's structure.

Step two: Create the book proposal. A book proposal replaces the structure phase of the process. The proposal is like the business plan for your book, and is valuable even if you want to publish independently. A complete proposal includes discussions of the target audience, the general theme and purpose of the book, and a chapter outline, table of contents, and sample chapter. It also covers marketing plans and market research.

For some authors, crafting the proposal is part of the creative process. Bestselling author Daniel Pink reports that he writes several book proposals in parallel to determine which topics he wants to work on.[1]

Step three: Incubate the book. In a slight variation on the standard seven steps, the incubation phase lands after the structure. Submitting a proposal to an agent or publisher creates a built-in delay, while you wait for a response. In practice, incubation continues through drafting.

Step four: Create the first draft. This step is a doozy, and it plays out differently depending on the author and the book. You may prefer to work sequentially through each chapter until you have a complete draft. Or, you may guide each chapter through outlining, drafting, and revision in turn. See the section that follows on "The Drafting Process."

Step five: Rest before revision. You will be ready for a break when you complete a first draft. However, deadlines may make you feel like you should start revising right away. Resist, even for a few days, in the name of sanity and perspective. Celebrate the completion of the first draft of the manuscript.

Step six: Revise. As with any writing, book revision is an iterative process. The length of a book means that each revision cycle takes longer. If you care deeply about the quality of the work, call on outside editors and proofreaders.

Step seven: Publish. Whether you operate independently or are working with a major publishing house, the time comes to pull the trigger and publish the book. Many months may elapse between this decision and the arrival of the book in the world. While you wait, it's time to start marketing—an entirely different topic.

The boundaries between these phases are fairly fluid for a book. Even as you draft, you may continue researching. If you undertake writing with a growth mindset, the outline often changes as you discover different approaches while developing the content.

Yet understanding the steps of the process helps you create a realistic schedule for the book and the work. With a schedule, you can track progress, remaining focused on the future so you can resist the temptations of the present. Following the process helps you manage the inevitable impatience and discouragement, balancing the need for speed with your desire for quality.

The Drafting Process

Once you hit the drafting phase of the book, the process folds back on itself, operating on a chapter-by-chapter or section-by-section level.

Individual parts, chapters, or sections traverse their own cycles, from research to outlining, drafting, and revision. The broad outline of the book doesn't always dictate exactly what happens within each chapter, leaving you with more structuring and outlining work.

Separate sections of the book may flow through the process at different rates, with staggered start times. Eventually, everything comes together into a draft that is ready for revision and publishing.

Some people approach drafting sequentially and logically, starting with the first chapter and working through to the last.

But there's a strong argument to be made for drafting chapters of nonfiction books in parallel, researching and outlining some sections while composing and revising others. Working in parallel gives you the ability to suit the work to your current mood and environment.

If you want to optimize writing productivity, set up the tasks so that you have the greatest chance of being productive on any given day.

If you feel unwell or don't have the uninterrupted time to achieve a state of flow, do other tasks instead. Research your topic or make notes of unresolved issues for incubation. When you're traveling, revising existing chapters may be easier than composing new text. With multiple sections of the book happening in parallel, you can direct your efforts based on your mood, abilities, and environment at the moment.

Readers travel from start to finish; authors can compose the draft in any order they like, and ensure linear consistency in revision. This holds true for fiction, even when the narrative flow or story arc is critical.

Joan Didion keeps story fragments pinned to a bulletin board in her office, hoping that they will find a home in the eventual novel as it progresses.

David Foster Wallace left his last work unfinished when he lost his life to depression in 2008. Best known for his 1,000+ page novel *Infinite Jest*, Wallace was in the midst of a novel titled *The Pale King*. The task of assembling the notes and drafts into a published book fell to Michael Pietsch, Wallace's editor at Little, Brown and Company.

In the preface of *The Pale King*, Pietsch describes sorting through printed manuscripts, binders, notebooks, notes, and lists when assembling the work to publish. Several sections were revised and polished, others lightly edited, and others very rough, with indications that Wallace planned to cut the text in half. And there were files filled with "zero drafts" or freewriting. Pietsch's observations offer a snapshot of this brilliant author's creative process; he worked on several parts of the book at the same time.

Use the seven-step process on the individual components of the book, in whatever order works best for you.

Staying the Course

I have a confession to make. When I was revising this chapter, a voice in my head said, "Maybe you don't need Part

Three of this book at all. Think of it—the book could be done right now, today." I stopped and considered it seriously for a few minutes. On the one hand, I felt that this chapter might be useful to a significant number of readers. On the other hand ... *I could be done!*

This thought popped into my head right after I'd finished working on the introduction to this chapter, describing the challenges of staying strong when faced with delayed gratification. Oh, the irony! Even when we understand the possible temptations rationally, we experience them anyway. My Muse felt ready to do something different. It was the perfect example of multiple selves in action.

Happily, I had a plan and a schedule for the book and knew that I could stick to it. My Scribe stayed the course, and these chapters are now here before you.

Schedules give us strength.

Revisiting the chapter on self-discipline and temptation, remember that well-spaced deadlines gave students a better shot at a good grade. Apply that lesson to your book.

Book deadlines are often vague and faraway objectives, such as "finish the book by the end of the year." Define the plan for how you're going to get there, week by week and step by step. Create a realistic but challenging schedule. Change it if you must, but maintain a schedule.

Minimum word count is a valuable measure, but it's not enough to plan your book.

If you want to write a book, you have no doubt heard variations on this theme: Simply write 1,000 words a day for two months, and you'll have 60,000 words—that's a legitimate book!

Well, sort of. It's 60,000 words.

Drafting is only one stage of writing. The complete process is much more than getting words on the page.

Word count is a false measure of progress if the words aren't the right words.

Decide on the overall schedule for the book itself: when you will have a proposal, a first draft, etc. Then set deadlines and objectives that are appropriate for each phase.

For example, perhaps you're working on three chapters at different phases: researching chapter three, outlining chapter two from the notes, and drafting chapter one. Word count objectives won't measure progress on days you outline or research.

Break down the book into tasks and define the required progress each day or week to ensure that the overall project advances toward completion.

Your objectives may vary from week to week. For example, you may choose to take each chapter through a cycle in sequence: research, outline, draft, and revise, then move on to the next chapter. In this example, completing one chapter every three weeks represents a reasonable measure of progress.

Because I like having work in multiple phases, I set both daily and weekly objectives for progress in the drafting phase; by the end of the week, I will have completed *this many* chapters and written *this many* words. One day may have a high word count, while the next I may spend hours revising. I can align my work with my mood and circumstances, with the knowledge that I'm working to a larger plan.

With a firm plan and goals, your mental state and environment can guide you to what you are most suited to do at a particular time. If you have ideas that you're ready to pursue in writing, put aside other activities and draft. If you cannot get into a good state of flow or the drafting is difficult, stop for the moment and research a later chapter; doing so may open doors for subsequent drafting. If you are out of chapters in the research and structure phase, alternate revision with drafting.

Having a plan with deadlines serves two important purposes. First, it improves productivity by combatting procrastination. Second, it forces you to show up and keep working even when the going is tough, and when obstacles to writing threaten.

---

[1] "How Bestselling Author Daniel Pink Writes," *The Writer Files* podcast, Rainmaker.FM, podcast episode 25 from July 27, 2015. Transcript available at rainmaker.fm/audio/writer/Daniel-pink-file.

Chapter 22

Lessons from Writing about Writing

I started this endeavor with an understanding of my own process and an interest in exploring how it fit with both cognitive science and the practices of other authors. In the course of analyzing the process of writing, my own methods have evolved.

Psychologists use the word *metacognition* (essentially "thinking about thinking") to describe awareness of our own thought processes. Metacognition has the potential to change our behavior. If we understand the flawed shorthand abstractions, heuristics, or mental shortcuts we use to make decisions, we can improve those processes, inviting the rational mind to weigh in.

Similarly, working on this book has been an exercise in *metawriting*. As I researched and drafted, my process has shifted, generally for the better. I have become more disciplined about certain aspects of my writing life, and have adopted habits learned from other authors. Here are a few lessons from my own journey.

The Muse is waiting. Although incubation has always been part of my process, since writing this book I have approached this phase as an intentional practice. I identify unresolved issues to consider before heading off to the gym or stopping for the night. And, like magic, answers or ideas appear when needed. Problems and puzzles no longer feel like obstacles; instead, they are welcome opportunities to explore unseen mental circuitry.

The Muse waits, on standby, for an invitation to participate in the work.

There's always room to improve the process. Before setting out to write, I considered myself a highly productive writer. But since exploring this topic, I have discovered ways to make the work more fluid and fun. Inspired by John Steinbeck's diaries, I've started a "prewriting" online journal entry every morning, which sets the course for the day and clarifies my thinking.

After hearing Sherry Turkle speak about the incursions of social media into solitude, I've become more diligent about delaying email until I've done an hour of work and keeping the phone at a distance during drafting. It's easy to backslide into checking email and frittering away time online; constant vigilance is the key.

Self-knowledge is the best defense. During the period of intense focus on this book, I encountered most of the hurdles that appear in part three, including the Imposter Syndrome, a bad cold, and assorted work-related crises. In other words, I had the opportunity to develop persistence by powering through the bad days.

It didn't feel so empowering when I was in the midst of them.

At one point, I almost stopped writing, thinking, *So many others have already written about writing already—who am I to contribute anything?* I was more than halfway through the draft. Lucky for me, I had my notes on the Imposter Syndrome handy, and kept writing.

I'm sure I'll keep learning. If you want to continue to explore the inner game of writing along with me, sign up for the Writing Process list at annejanzer.com. In the Resources section of the website, you can find information related to this book, including a quick reference for the seven-step writing recipe.

The work of honing one's craft is never finished—neither is the inner game of being a writer.

Acknowledgments

In discussing the inner game of writing, I have neglected one of the most important parts of the writing process: finding support from those around you.

When it comes to keeping your brain in gear, the support and assistance of others is invaluable. Perhaps I should write a book about assembling the team to support the inner game of writing. I have been extremely lucky in this regard. In lieu of a new book, here are a few, insufficient words of gratitude.

I am indebted to the numerous authors and writers who have shared with me their individual stories. Some, like Deborah Underwood, are quoted in the text. For every individual author mentioned, dozens others have offered their experiences and insights in conversations, helping me to understand what we share and where we differ. I'm grateful for each and every conversation.

Early readers have provided valuable insight that has led to marked improvements in the book. Among them, Corrie

Ann Gray and Roger C. Parker have made suggestions at precisely the point I needed them. Roger has contributed as well by sharing his interviews with other authors, alongside his own experiences.

The book has benefited from other intrepid guides on its path to publication. Holly Brady has been a constant source of advice through all of my publishing-related endeavors. Thomas McGee of Rightly Designed always finds exactly the right image and feel for a book cover. And I put this book before you with greater confidence after submitting the text to the professional eyes and exquisite language sensitivities of Laurie Gibson and Mark Rhynsburger for copyediting and proofreading. Any mistakes remaining are my own, undoubtedly introduced after their careful examination.

A small army of friends and colleagues has helped me put this book out into the world, sharing reviews and insight. I am grateful to each and every one; naming them all would seriously inflate the page count of this book.

Above all, the ongoing support, guidance, and advice of my family make it possible for my Muse and Scribe to work together with some degree of sanity. I'm entirely indebted to the unending patience, support, and wise advice of my husband Steve.

Glossary

These are a few of the terms that appear throughout the book.

Abundance mindset: The belief that a resource (ideas, marshmallows, money) exists in sufficient quantities that one does not need to carefully meter, hoard, or protect it. (See the scarcity mindset for its opposite.)

Attention: The connection between our inner selves and the outer world.

Curse of Knowledge: The challenge of imagining the perspective of someone who lacks your knowledge or understanding.

Empathy: The ability to share or understand another person's experiences or feelings.

Fixed mindset: The perspective that performance is a product of fixed abilities or talents.

Flow: A state of effortless attention in which one loses track of time and is completely absorbed in the task at hand without self-consciousness or fear.

Focus: The act of directing attention; in most cases, focus refers to the intentional and targeted deployment of attention to a specific activity or task.

Growth mindset: The belief that one can control one's own performance and expand abilities through growth and learning.

Imposter Syndrome: The mistaken belief sometimes held by accomplished individuals that they will be discovered as frauds; an inability to internalize one's own abilities and accomplishments.

Incubation: A stage in the creative process in which the subconscious mind works on a problem or issue, seemingly without conscious effort.

Incubation Effect: The observed effect in which people are more creative when their brains are given a chance to work on a problem in the background.

Metacognition: Thinking about thinking.

Mindset: A set of acting assumptions and attitudes that influence behavior.

Multitasking: Doing more than one thing at once. From a neuroscience perspective, multitasking is a mirage. In reality, you're switching your focus back and forth very quickly.

Muse: In this book, the Muse refers to the parts of the brain involved with intuition, subconscious connections, and other thought processes that happen outside of conscious control.

Negativity bias: The mental tendency to give negative thoughts or responses more mental weight and focus than neutral or positive ones.

Open attention: A state in which the thinking mind wanders, without focusing on anything in particular. In open attention, the Muse has a chance to be heard. You may experience open attention when engaged in simple, everyday activities that require little directed focus.

Resilience: The ability to recover from or adjust to negative occurrences and setbacks.

Scarcity mindset: The perception that a resource is fixed and finite, insufficient to meet everyone's needs. When nine hungry people are presented with eight pieces of pie, the scarcity mindset will most likely result. The opposite is an abundance mindset.

Scribe: I use this term to refer to the mental systems that use deliberate, intentional thought, effort, and discipline. In times before the printing press, scribes performed the essential work of copying and writing books.

System 1 and System 2: Daniel Kahneman refers to these two systems in decision making. System 1 is intuitive and automatic, relying on shortcuts to save us the work of analysis. System 2 uses deliberate and intentional thought.

Zeigarnick Effect: The brain's tendency to reserve processing for unresolved issues: this contributes to *incubation*.

Index

About the Author

Anne Janzer is an award-winning author and nonfiction writing coach on a mission to help people communicate more effectively through writing.

As a professional writer and marketing consultant, she has worked with more than a hundred technology companies to articulate positioning and messages in crowded markets.

Her other books include *Writing to Be Understood: What Works and Why*, *Subscription Marketing*, and *The Workplace Writer's Process*. You can access her blog posts and online courses on her website, AnneJanzer.com.

For updates on her ongoing search for a better writing process, or to subscribe to the Writing Practices weekly emails, visit AnneJanzer.com.

Made in the USA
Monee, IL
29 May 2020